The Department of Defense and Homeland Security

A Monograph
by
Major Timothy McAteer
United States Army

MENS EST CLAVIS VICTORIAE

School of Advanced Military Studies
United States Army Command and General Staff College
Fort Leavenworth, Kansas
AY 01-02

SCHOOL OF ADVANCED MILITARY STUDIES

MONOGRAPH APPROVAL

Timothy J. McAteer Major, U.S. Army

Title of Monograph: The Department of Defense and Homeland Security

Approved by:

_____   Monograph Director
Dr. Robert Epstein

_____   Professor and Director
Robert H. Berlin, Ph.D.   Academic Affairs,
                                             School of Advanced
                                             Military Studies

_____   Director, Graduate Degree
Philip J. Brookes, Ph.D.   Program

Abstract

The Department of Defense and Homeland Security by Major Timothy McAteer, 63 pages.

It is quite possible that after the events of 11 September 2001, the roles and missions of the Department of Defense in the area of Homeland Security are destined for change. This monograph provides and examination of the legal, and traditional aspects of Homeland Security in the U.S. and the current framework for managing a domestic Weapons of Mass Destruction (WMD) incident. Understanding the past roles and missions of the DoD in regard to Homeland Security are relevant as the Office of Homeland Security (OHS) formulates a comprehensive national strategy for Homeland Security. Throughout the Nation's history, the American public has consistently equated Homeland Security with the Armed Forces. Immediately following the 11 September attacks there was confusion among many in the U.S. government as to which federal agency was responsible for Homeland Security. Several key members of the Senate Armed Services committee expressed concern over the current security framework and the DoD's supporting role in domestic Homeland Security. This monograph addresses these issues through an examination of the DoD's (Armed Forces) historical role in the defense of the nation as well as its role in domestic support operations.

The monograph begins with a brief analysis of the emerging threats that the United States faces, and offers a proposed definition for Homeland Security. This is followed by an examination of the evolution of legal considerations when employing federal military forces in a domestic support capacity. It addresses the Posse Comitatus Act and recent refinements to the Act that circumvent its provisions in instances of clearly identified threats to the Nation's interests. The second chapter includes an analysis of Civil Defense and the DoD's participation in past Civil Defense missions. A chronology of Civil Defense in America is included beginning with post World War I activities up through the present time. This analysis illustrates that in time of crisis, when the public feels vulnerable, they look to the DoD for security. The monograph outlines the current DoD supporting role to both the FBI for Crisis Management and to the FEMA for Consequence Management during a WMD incident. The monograph argues that the current system is adequate and the DoD should not be designated as the LFA for WMD incidents.

The monograph recommends the creation of a new Commander-in-Chief (CINC) for Homeland Security. This CINC should also be charged with the responsibility of developing the campaign for, and executing the global War on Terror. Additional recommendations include some minor changes to both Joint and Army doctrine in regard to Homeland Security. It also recommends that the DoD maintain a receptive attitude towards new domestic missions, advocating the temporary execution of non-traditional missions.

TABLE OF CONTENTS

Introduction

On 11 September 2001, the United States of America (U.S.A.) found itself on the losing end of the first battle, of its first war in the 21st century. The terrorist attacks upon the World Trade Center Towers in New York City and The Pentagon in Washington D.C. achieved complete surprise and shocked the entire structure of the U.S.A. homeland. In less than ninety minutes, a group of 19 men operating at the tactical level inflicted calamitous damage to the nation. The toll of the attack was staggering: including more than two-thousand nine hundred people killed, complete destruction of the World Trade Center complex, a week long closure of the New York world financial district, suspension of all commercial aircraft flights, and significant destruction of the Pentagon. There were more people killed in The Pentagon attack, considered the lesser of the 11 September targets, than were lost in combat during the entire Persian Gulf War.[1] Added to the horrific events of the day was unprecedented intense and timely media coverage, the vast majority of the population watched most of the carnage in real time. The long term toll of the attacks upon the American psyche remains to be seen but there is no doubt that 11 September 2001 was without question one of the most momentous days in the history of the Nation. A very common question that citizens across the U.S.A. asked, as they watched the World Trade Center Towers collapse and the Pentagon burn was, "How could this happen here?"

In the days that followed 11 September, as the reality of events began to sink in, Americans from all walks of life began looking for explanations. Many questions focused on one obvious point, which was the complete inability of the federal government to protect its citizens and institutions from this devastating assault. The unfortunate truth is that the most powerful military

---

[1] Cheney, R. "Vice President Cheney Delivers remarks at the 56th Annual Alfred E. Smith Memorial Foundation Dinner" (speech given at the Waldorf-Astoria Hotel, N.Y.C.18 October 2001) Internet. Available from:www.whitehouse.gov/vicepresident/.com Accessed 5 January 2002.

defense establishment ever assembled on earth could do nothing to stop these attacks; it could only offer assistance in cleaning up the damage. The Secretary of Defense, Donald Rumsfeld and the Department of Defense (DoD), which he leads, could not escape the intense scrutiny of the public's demand for answers. Appearing on ABC News' Sunday morning talk show 'This Week', just five days after the attack, reporter Sam Donaldson asked Secretary Rumsfeld the following question. "To what extent is the U.S. military today… prepared to meet an attack like the one that came last Tuesday?" The Secretary replied,

> Under our Constitution, under our laws, the United States military's task is to defend against foreign invasions and foreign threats. The threat we saw recently was from a person in our own country in one of our airplanes filled with our citizens. This is a law enforcement job. It is a job for the Federal Bureau of Investigation (FBI). It is a job for the police… And we have a whole set of arrangements and rules that have existed since (for) decades. And what we need to do and what we are doing is to review those and ask ourselves how we have to shift our arrangements. [2]

Upon initial examination, it is somewhat disconcerting that the Secretary of Defense would make such a statement on the heels of the single most destructive attack experienced in the last 150 years of the United States' existence. Taken literally, his statement suggests that somehow the Defense Department did not bear partial responsibility for the failure of protecting the Nation from the 11 September attack. Is it unreasonable for the average citizen to have the expectation that an inherent task of the DoD is to prevent the events like those of 11 September?[3] Powerful voices in The United States Congress have the same expectations of the DoD and feel that the time has come for the DoD to take the role of Lead Federal Agency (LFA) on the domestic front in the war against terror. Senator Max Cleland (D-GA), a member of the Senate

---

[2] Donald Rumsfeld, interviewed by Sam Donaldson, "ABC News This Week" 16 September 2001.
[3] Ikle, Fred C. "Defending the U.S. Homeland Strategic and Legal Issues for DOD and the Armed Services" CSIS Homeland Defense Working Group January 1999. pg. 9. The author, in 1999, offers a logical argument concerning the public's expectations of who should defend the U.S. "It stands to reason that we, as Americans, would expect and demand that our armed forces defend our own homeland against attacks worse than Pearl Harbor. Indeed, it would seem politically unacceptable for the president to let the attorney general and the director of the FBI be in charge of defending the nation, with the National Guard and perhaps some specialized units of the army and marine corps merely helping with first aid and cleanup."

Armed Services Committee stated in hearings on 25 October 2001,

> " I don't think we need much more evidence to understand that we're not…in a crime scene here…This is war. So I am not quite comfortable with the FBI leading the war against terrorism and being the lead agency…If we are in a war, I think the Department of Defense ought to be the lead dog here….I think the number one agency in the defense of America is the Defense Department.".[4]

However, an in-depth review of Mr. Rumsfeld's comments reveals that he was correct in his understanding of the DoD's domestic role in the immediate aftermath of the events of 11 September. He accurately expressed the traditional and accepted legal and operational framework of the Nation's security structure. The question now becomes, is it time to change the status quo concerning DoD's roles and missions on the domestic front in light of the new and emerging threats to the Nation's security?

Purpose

The purpose of this monograph is to examine DoD roles, missions, tasks and interagency responsibilities in the domestic area of operations, primarily in response to a domestic terrorist attacks employing Weapons of Mass Destruction (WMD). The focus of this monograph is therefore limited to the domestic realm of Homeland Security. The ongoing war on terrorism that is currently underway in various locations around the globe, involving primarily DoD assets, is inextricably linked to the overall security of the Nation. However, those actions are beyond the scope of this monograph. The domestic employment, legality, organization, and command and control of DoD assets in this new war will be the principal areas of concern here. It is time to examine past and current strategies, policies, organizations, interagency coordination and legal requirements, in hope of identifying possible areas of improvement domestically. The end state of this analysis must be a national security structure that effectively and efficiently employs DoD assets in the proper time and space in order to sufficiently protect the homeland while preserving

---

[4] "U.S. Senator Carl Levin (D-MI) Senate Armed Services Committee, Holds Hearing on the Department of Defense's Role in Homeland Security." *FDCH Political Transcripts*, 10/25/01, Washington DC. Pg 13.

the long-standing relationship between U.S. citizens and their military. Additionally, it might become apparent that the current systems in place are quite adequate and require only minor modifications, as opposed to wholesale re-invention in order for the DoD to sufficiently support domestic security missions.

In the weeks and months immediately following 11 September, emotions were running extremely high throughout the government, military and other agencies that felt to some extent culpable for their failure to protect the Nation. This is understandable, but emotional responses often do not lead to the creation of the most prudent and potentially effective strategies. Visible, highly publicized change does not always equal improvement. Perhaps DoD does not need to expand its current position in domestic operations. The title of Lead Federal Agency (LFA) might best be suited for domestic law enforcement agencies. Some might feel that by showing change, the DoD and the federal government is showing progress. This is not always the case. The aim herein is to examine the complex nature of the current situation at the strategic and operational levels and determine what and how the DOD should contribute to the Homeland Security mission.

Methodology

This monograph begins by providing some essential definitions and a brief explanation of the potential threats aimed at the U.S.A. The first chapter is devoted to a historical analysis of the traditional and legal role of federal military forces employed in domestic support operations. Chapter 2 analyzes the DoD's role in Civil Defense in America, and highlights some of the similarities between Homeland Security and Civil Defense. The third chapter outlines the formulation and development of the current federal interagency process for managing the effects of a WMD attack, and DoD's responsibilities within that process. The monograph concludes with a summation of the presented information and recommendations for the employment of DoD assets in support of civil authorities during a domestic WMD attack and in support of the Homeland Security strategy.

Definitions

Immediately after the 11 September attack, defining and explaining the differences

between Homeland Security and Homeland Defense became very important. Multitudes of

experts and pundits were using these words and terms interchangeably and many times

incorrectly. A start point for any useful discussion on this topic requires a common lexicon. It is

extremely important to agree on definitions to avert confusion from the outset.[5] As unbelievable

as it might sound, definitions for the terms Homeland Security and Homeland Defense do not

appear in the Department of Defense Dictionary of Military and Associated Terms, Joint

Publication 1-02.[6] For the purposes of this monograph, the following definition of Homeland

Security is offered for consideration:

> Homeland Security refers to the interagency efforts to secure the
> population and key institutions of the United States from terrorist attacks. This
> includes: preparing for, detecting, deterring, and pre-empting such attacks, while
> also employing the capability to manage the consequences of an attack in order
> to mitigate prolonged effects. While the primary focus of Homeland Security
> activities is the protection of citizens and assets against acts of terror within the
> geographical confines of the United States, the means to attain this end might
> well be employed beyond the physical borders of the Nation.[7]

The above definition is broad enough to ensure that the entire responsibility of Homeland

Security does not fall completely on the shoulders of the DoD. This is an important distinction

from the current definitions employed by many in the DoD. This proposed definition is designed

to encompass every aspect of this complex task while not assigning any undertaking to a

---

[5] Department of Defense, *Quadrennial Defense Review Report*, 30 September 2001. Pg. 19.

[6] Dobbs Michael, CDR, USN, "Homeland Security: New Challenges for an Old Responsibility" *ANSER Journal of Homeland Security*, March 2001. Internet. Available from www homelandsecurity.org/ journal/articles/displayArticle.asp?article=4. Accessed 10 February 2002.

[7] This definition is a compilation from three sources, first is the OHS mission statement, which specifies protection from terrorist attacks. Internet Available from: www.whitehouse.gov/news/releases/2001. Accessed 8 October 2001. Second is from a proposed definition in the Rand Study *Preparing the U.S. Army for Homeland Security, Concepts, Issues, and Options*, which is too narrow and focuses primarily on 'military' activities as opposed to a broader interagency approach, the third is from CDR Dobbs' article "Homeland Security: New Challenges for an Old Responsibility" This is a bit broad it focuses on any act of aggression targeted against the U.S. None of the cited definitions included the concept that in order to achieve complete Homeland Security, activities must be conducted abroad as well as domestically. Any definition that focuses only on the domestic or military aspects of this mission is not sufficient.

particular agency.

The term 'Homeland Defense', from a DoD perspective, describes what might be characterized as the more traditional function of the military. For the purpose of this monograph, it includes the protection of the United States from attack from more conventional threats from aerospace, land, sea, or through computer network attacks. The key thing to remember is that the two terms are closely related and interdependent. However, they are not synonymous. This monograph will focus its attention primarily on Homeland Security matters.

As members of the Office of Homeland Security (OHS) begin to develop a comprehensive Homeland Security strategy, they must not approach it with any preconceived ideas of exactly who does what. Instead, as the strategy begins to take form, it is clear that at its center will be the potential threats to the nation. The threat of terrorists employing weapons of mass destruction (WMD) needs to be number one on the list.

Threat Overview

A detailed and comprehensive examination of the current terrorist threat is well beyond the scope of this monograph. This portion is included in order to establish a framework from which to study Homeland Security. A start point for any serious discussion about Homeland Security must begin with an understanding of the enemy and the new area of operations. Only when one understands the threat and terrorist methods of operation, can a truly critical examination of the current security constructs be achieved. The operational environment is changing. The United States' geographic isolation no longer provides a buffer from the outside world.

The enemy in this war is extremely motivated, capable, and is undoubtedly living among the American people, looking for weakness and planning his next attack. The threat of a terrorist organization conducting another domestic attack utilizing some form of a WMD is almost a certainty. The pattern of escalating terrorist audacity and rhetoric, the availability of WMD components, the vulnerability of the United States' electronic networks and the openness and freedoms of U.S. society all add up to a very real chance for disaster. The DoD's role in defeating this agile enemy and securing the homeland is no easy task.

Several events in the 1990's focused the attention of many officials in the government of the United States onto the topic of protecting the Nation from terrorist attacks. The World Trade Center bombing in 1993, the Murrah Federal Building Bombing in Oklahoma City in 1995, and the actions of the Aum Shinrikyo cult, who released chemical agents in a Tokyo subway system in 1995, each were events that highlighted the Nation's domestic vulnerabilities, and displayed a newfound boldness by the perpetrators of terror. The Clinton administration took notice and began to take steps towards better preparing the nation to effectively deal with a major terrorist attack (a detailed analysis of these steps is provided in a subsequent chapter). The most troublesome terrorist threats identified were ones that envisioned the employment of a weapon of mass destruction (WMD) in a heavily populated urban area.[8] A WMD can take many forms. The most common are: chemical, biological, radiological, nuclear, and high yield explosives. These types of WMD are often collectively described using the single acronym of CBRNE. The second type of attack that causes great concern is the threat of computer or electronic network attacks aimed at critical electronic infrastructure systems, often referred to as Weapons of Mass Disruption.

The proliferation of WMD capabilities, coupled with the ability to rapidly gather and pass information makes locating and interdicting WMD components difficult.[9] These weapons are accessible to terrorists and will undoubtedly be a part of the military and defense landscape well into the future. The likelihood of another attack using some form of a WMD on American soil is still very high. As stated in the U.S. Commission on National Security/21st Century,

> The combination of unconventional weapons proliferation with the
> persistence of international terrorism will end the relative invulnerability of the

---

[8] Larson and Peters, 54.

[9] Schweitzer, Glenn E. with Dorsch, Carole. *Superterrorism, Assassins, Mobsters, and Weapons of Mass Destruction* Plenum Trade: New York. Pgs 51-164.

U.S. homeland to catastrophic attack. A direct attack against American citizens on American soil is likely over the next quarter century…In the face of this threat, our nation has no coherent or integrated governmental structures.[10]

The fact that the U.S. endured one attack on 11 September 2001 does not mean in any way, shape, or form that the Nation is now immune. As the U.S. prosecutes the war against terror abroad, many of the enemy's motivations are subsequently increased. This raises the likely hood of another attack on American soil, perhaps using a WMD. A recent Government Accounting Office study stated that, "The United States…face(s) increasingly diffuse threats in the post-cold War era. In the future, potential adversaries are more likely to strike vulnerable civilian or military forces on the battlefield."[11] The availability of WMD components is frightening. Numerous examples exist of improperly secured nuclear materials and unemployed scientists within the former Soviet Union who have WMD experience and who are willing to sell their knowledge.[12] The threat is very real, and as the existing War on Terror continues, it is only logical that the enemy will eventually regroup and strike back. The worst thing to do now is to lose the sense of urgency that prevails. The terrorists are patient. The first attack on the World Trade Center Towers was in 1993, and the next was eight and a half years later. There are those that discount the effectiveness or likelihood of employment of WMD other then the high explosive type.[13] Several authors also claim that the reason there are so few examples of chemical-bio terrorism is due to the technical complexity involved in acquiring and delivering them.[14] The tone of their arguments is almost condescending towards the enemy, suggesting that

---

[10] The United States Commission on National Security/21st Century (Hart/Rudmann) Phase III report, Pg ii. 15 February 2001.

[11] GAO-02-160T Homeland Security challenges and Strategies in Addressing Short-and Long –Term National Needs pp 3.

[12] Lake, Anthony. *6 Nightmares Real Threats in A Dangerous World and How America Can Meet Them.* Little Brown and Company: 2001. (Pgs 24-32) An excellent synopsis of WMD component availability and cited examples of foiled WMD component procurement and movement.

[13] Claridge, David. "Exploding the Myths of Superterrorism, " in *The Future of Terrorism* ed. Taylor, Max and Horgan John. Ed. London: Cass Publishers, 2000, 133-48.

[14] Weiss, Aaron. "When Terror Strikes Who Should Respond?" *Parameters,* Autumn 2001, 124-5.

most terrorist organizations are too inept to pull off a sophisticated attack using biological or chemical agents.

The bio-terrorism attacks in September and October 2001, using the U.S. Postal Service as a delivery means for deadly Anthrax thoroughly refutes their premise. Although it did not cause thousands of causalities, the event did exhibit how relatively simple it is to spread certain agents. These Anthrax attacks did cause some lose of life and disrupted several government functions including closure of several government offices and the suspension of a meeting of Congress. The 1993 World Trade Center attack also had the potential to be a successful chemical attack. The explosives were configured with sodium cyanide, which fortunately burned off, rather than vaporizing.[15] Ignoring these weapons and the terrorists' desire and capability to employ them is naïve. The last point to mention concerning the threat is that the enemy faced today is one that has proven to be very adaptive, patient and committed to achieving their goals, no matter how long it takes. Just as the U.S. military learns from its past operations, so do the enemies of the U.S.A.

A recent article in *Military Review* outlines how after the Oklahoma City Bombing the FBI devised new methods to track the purchase of potentially hazardous materials. Prospective terrorists adapted their methodology, which led to increased incidents of smuggling of these items into the country. This change was met with a corresponding increase in border security activities. The enemy then adapted again in order to overcome U.S. counteractions. "Recognizing this new factor in the security environment, the methodology was again modified, this time creating the kinetic effect of explosives-a fully fueled, large aircraft-without the inherent intelligence indicators that would compromise the attack while, bypassing personnel and vehicle control

---

[15] Sentencing Statement of Judge J Duffy who presided over the trials of the 1993 WTC attackers. "Not only had they attempted to topple the north tower into the south tower…but they also planned to unleash a poison gas attack. Had the sodium cyanide packed in with the explosives not burned…but vaporized the cyanide gas would have been sucked into the North Tower." U.S. Senate. Permanent Sub Committee on Investigations of the Committee of Govt. Affairs Global Proliferation of WMD, Part III, Mar 27, 1996.

measures at the World Trade Center implemented after the 1993 attack.[16] The terrorists were able to adapt their methods to meet U.S. responses to their most recent actions. They appear to be a step ahead and capable of retaining the initiative in many cases. It also appears that another adaptation is the seemingly arbitrary nature of the attacks. "Rather than a fixed capability looking for an opportunity, the threat appears to be designing the capability to attack assessed vulnerabilities."[17] An example of the terrorists' ability to adapt might manifest itself in the following manner.

After the federal government develops and refines the capability to defend and respond to attacks in the large cities of the nation, the enemy might very well attack a smaller, more vulnerable target. If the enemy's purpose is to kill American's and have that action broadcast across the world via the international media, he is in a target rich environment anywhere in the U.S.A. Within hours if not minutes, any WMD attack targeting civilians in the U.S.A. will be 'Breaking News'. From the enemy's perspective, why attack a high school on a military base that is access controlled and surrounded by

gates when one can go two miles down the road and destroy a similar target that is not guarded? Why conduct a biological or chemical attack against a major urban area, which is better prepared to deal with it, as opposed to attacking a town of three thousand residents with no response capability. These are only a sampling of the potential threat scenarios that face the U.S.A. and as officials improve systems to counter, the enemy adapts and attacks the weakest spot. This can make developing security measures quite demanding.

The terrorist threat that the United States faces is quite different from anything ever dealt with before. The potential for a WMD attack on U.S. soil is extremely high and the commonly

---

[16] Shaughnessy, David and Cowan, Thomas "Attack on America: The First War of the 21st Century" *Military Review* November-December 2001, 3.
[17] Ibid., 3.

used phrase of "not if, but when an attack occurs" is still very applicable.[18] Understanding the

threat, including its capabilities and vulnerabilities, is essential to defeating it. It is also essential

in DoD's development of a strategy to support domestic operations in the aftermath of a WMD

attack in the U.S.A.

---

[18] Larson and Peters. Pg 54. The author's offer a probability matrix for the likelihood of a WMD attack within the next ten years. Their model is based on 25 terrorist groups with a .01 chance per annum of acquiring and employing a WMD. The probability of a successful attack in next year $(1-(1-0.01)^{25})=.222$, a 1/5 probability. Over the next ten years $(1-(1-0.01)^{25x10})=.918$ a nine in ten probability.

Chapter 1 Legal Considerations

Introduction

Before the attacks of 11 September, the lines that divided federal agency responsibilities and missions during a domestic WMD attack or incident were very clear. The Department of Justice (DOJ), through the Federal Bureau of Investigation (FBI) was designated as Lead Federal Agency (LFA) for crisis management. Crisis Management includes all activities aimed at detecting and defeating a WMD terrorist attack before it occurs, as well as conducting the criminal investigation, apprehension and prosecution of suspects after said incidents; and other primarily law enforcement-type activities. The Federal Emergency Management Agency (FEMA) had been designated LFA for Consequence Management. Consequence Management includes all the efforts of state, local and federal efforts to mitigate damage of a WMD incident and restore pre-attack conditions. The DoD was designated as a support agency to the FBI for Crisis Management and to FEMA for Consequence Management, the latter receiving the majority of effort by the DoD.[19]

Since 11 September, these dividing lines are not as clearly defined. In October 2001, by Executive Order 13228, the President established the Office of Homeland Security (OHS) and the Homeland Security Council (HSC). This office falls within the Executive Branch and is headed by the Assistant to the President for Homeland Security. The overall purpose of the OHS is to "…develop and coordinate the implementation of a comprehensive national strategy to secure the United States from terrorist threats or attacks."[20]

It is too early to determine the amount of influence that the OHS will have on the DoD, but it is clear that some missions of the DoD are likely to change. This is already evident by the ongoing

---

[19] CONPLAN, United States Government Interagency Domestic Terrorism Concept of Operations Plan
[20] Bush, George W. "Executive Order 13228". *Weekly Compilation of Presidential Documents*, Vol. 37, Issue 41, pp1434. 15 October 2001.

domestic operations that DoD is leading since 11 September. A portion of these missions include: combat air patrols under the operational control of NORAD, National Guard soldiers in a non-federal status conducting airport security, and most recently, the federalization of additional National Guard soldiers to assist Border Patrol operations. What is unique about this latest requirement is that these National Guard soldiers are serving in a federal status.

This use of these federal assets to support the DOJ's Border Patrol, the Immigration and Naturalization Service (INS) and the Treasury Department's Customs Service is a significant departure from past practices.[21] Additionally, in the conduct of their duties, these federalized National Guard military forces will support law enforcement agencies, but they will not carry weapons. This example highlights many of the issues resulting from the use of military forces in domestic operations within the new operating environment.

The problems of when and where to employ federal military forces in domestic situations are complex. The traditional school of thought had been that the DoD's focus should reside primarily on foreign threats and that any assistance to civilian or domestic agencies was a secondary task. These old paradigms are grounded in a foundation of precedent, law and tradition. After 11 September, the rules changed, and so has DoD's role. As the relevancy of past security and defense systems are reviewed in light of these new circumstances, it is important to understand how the current division of authority between federal agencies, relevant to this issue evolved to where it is today.

Military Forces and the Constitution

At the heart of this issue is the question, "What is the primary purpose of the U.S. government, and how should the DoD support the attainment of that end?" The most basic and logical place to find the answer to that question is in the Constitution of the United States. The

---

[21] "Debate Swells Over Sending Unarmed Troops to Guard U.S. Borders" Inside the Pentagon. March 7 2002. Internet. Available from: http://ebird.dtic.mil/Mar2002/e20020307debate htm. Accesses on 10 March 2002.

Preamble to the Constitution outlines some overarching roles of the federal government. It part it states,

> In order to form a more perfect Union, establish justice, insure domestic Tranquility, provide for the common defense, promote the general welfare, and secure the Blessings of Liberty to ourselves and our Posterity.

This portion of the Preamble has definite implications for the basic role of U.S. military forces as a subset of the federal government. The context in which the framers drafted the Constitution is one that requires a brief examination. In 1787, the framers clearly understood that the prospect of forming and maintaining a solid allegiance of the thirteen colonies under a single, federal system was tenuous at best. They faced several challenges and the most daunting was the ability of the nation to secure itself. There were both internal and external prevailing threats. There was also fear that disunion among the colonies would lead to European intervention, causing a "duplication of Europe all over again, with shifting alliances and alignments, standing military forces, wars and competition for dominance."[22] There were foreign threats against the coast and ports of the Union. Being a maritime nation, the government at the time had to address these threats in order to ensure economic progress through foreign trade. Internally, the two major threats were insurrection and Native Americans who inhabited the continent.

Militias and Congressional Power

The framers knew that in order to maintain the union they had to defend it on two fronts, both the foreign and domestic. However, many citizens distrusted and feared a strong central government that had at its disposal a standing military instrument. The public's apprehension towards a full-time, federally-controlled military was an ingrained part of the American psyche. It had grown out of the idea that any leader with an army at his disposal would undoubtedly evolve into military despotism. This fear was eclipsed by the events of January 1787, when

---

[22] Kohn, Richard, "The Constitution and National Security" The *United States Military Under the Constitution of the United States*, 1789-1989. 65-6.

Daniel Shays, a former Continental captain led a revolt in Massachusetts. This action, known as Shays Rebellion, which was eventually subdued, highlighted the weaknesses of the Confederation as well as Congress' inability to suppress insurrectionist activities that had lasted for more than six months.[23]

The events of Shays Rebellion shocked many of the early political leaders of the U.S. As they assembled at the Constitutional Convention in the same year, the memory of Shays' foray, and the government's complete inability to react to it, was still fresh in their minds. They knew that they had to form a mechanism to provide a coercive capability to the central government if other methods failed. The ability to secure the Union had to be balanced with the recognized fear and distrust of standing armies, created by decades of British rule. The primary argument designed to quell that fear and support increased federal power was offered by the Federalists, who understood the importance of a central government capable of providing much-needed security while maintaining a semblance of rights for the individual states. The national system envisioned by both Alexander Hamilton and James Madison provided a balancing effect for a central power to exert itself first through law first and then by force only as a last resort, envisioning that, "law and force could operate together to compel compliance without tearing society apart."[24] A goal of the Constitutional Convention in 1787 was to address these issues. The most important outcome of the Constitutional Convention, from a military perspective, was the power granted to the Congress, "To raise and support armies, To provide and maintain a navy and To provide for calling forth the Militia to execute Laws of the Union, suppress Insurrections and repel invasions."[25] Additionally, it was at this time that the President was designated as the Commander in Chief, placing the military firmly under civilian control, easing civilian

---

[23] Urwin, Gregory J.W. The Army of the Constitution: The Historical Context, "…*To ensure domestic Tranquility, provide for the common defense …Papers from the Conference on Homeland Protection.*" Strategic Studies Institute. ed. Manwaring, Max G. October, 2000, 28-36.
[24] Ibid., 67. Hamilton, Alexander, "Federalist Paper Number 16" as cited in Kohn's article.
[25] U.S. Constitution , Article I section 8.

apprehension of a British style military construct. These powers to the President and Congress mark the beginning of a federal force, subordinate to civilian authority, designed to protect the security of the federal government and the Union itself. Subsequent statutes created the Secretary of Defense and the various service secretaries. This served to further formalize and organize the basic principle of civilian control of military forces within the U.S.

Domestic Military Operations

In the years that followed the Constitutional Convention, the U.S. government employed federalized militia on several occasions. The most serious test to the fledgling democracy came soon after the Convention, in the form of The Whiskey Rebellion. This 1794 event required the use of 'called up' state militias to form and move to the Appalachian Mountains to subdue farmers that refused to pay a whiskey tax levied by Congress. President Washington attempted to negotiate a settlement, but eventually resorted to committing troops. He urged restraint by the military forces, sensitive to the perception of federalized forces crushing discontent.[26] In the end, the rebellion fizzled out before armed confrontation, but there were some important lessons learned. Of particular importance was the fact that it had taken more than a month to mobilize the militias and then commit them to action.[27] This led to the continued maintenance of a small; full-time federal military, but the mainstay of defense and security remained the militia.

In the 19th and 20th centuries, the use of federalized forces to support civilian authority, enforce federal law or support state requests for intervention can best be categorized as episodic. After The Whiskey rebellion, up through the Civil War, the primary use of federal forces in a domestic support role was to quell abolitionist uprisings both along the east coast and in the Kansas territory. The post-Civil War years saw the use of federal forces to facilitate Reconstruction policies in the South.

---

[26] Cooper Jerry M. "Federal Military Intervention," in *The United States Military Under the Constitution of the United States*, 1789-1989. ed. Kohn, Richard, (New York: NYU Press, 1991) , 125.
[27] Ibid., 123-36.

In the 1900s, troops were committed on numerous occasions to enforce federal laws and to subdue civil disturbance. In July, 1932, federal troops under the control of Douglas MacArthur forcibly removed World War I veterans known as the 'Bonus Marchers' from Washington D.C.[28] In the tumultuous decade of the 1960's, federal forces were employed on numerous occasions to support state and local governments. These deployments were primarily a result of social strife over the issues of desegregation, integration, anti-war protests and urban discontent.[29] These events became so frequent that the DoD established the Department of Defense Civil Disturbance Steering Committee. This committee, comprised of members of the JCS, DOJ, FBI and the White House, developed policies to address multiple concurrent instances of civil unrest.[30] Additionally, the Army began specific Civil Defense training for its senior officers at Fort Gordon Military Police School. During the Viet Nam War, "Army intelligence units conducted investigations against 100,000 Americans."[31] These activities, in part later led to Senate investigations (The Church Committee) that revealed the military's actions against U.S. citizens. "So damaging were the excesses exposed, the military's appetite for domestic security activities dampened markedly."[32]

Contemporary Operations

There are several examples since 1990, of deployments of federal troops in support of civilian agencies. In 1992, Joint Task Force Los Angeles (JTF-LA) was formed in response to intense rioting and civil unrest in Los Angeles, California following the unpopular Rodney King court ruling. In this case, United States Marines, Army soldiers and federalized California National Guard soldiers formed within 24 hours of the President's order to commit them to

---

[28] Perret, Geoffrey. *Old Soldiers Never Die* Pg 154-5.
[29] Cooper, 125-133.
[30] Cooper, 140.
[31] Johnson, Loch K. "Season of Inquiry", as cited in Dunlap, Charles " Where Domestic Security and Civil Liberties Collide" in *...to insure domestic Tranquility, provide for the common defence...* Manwaring ed. 213-223.
[32] Ibid., 213.

action. They were deployed and assisted local police authorities in restoring order.[33] In 1995, soldiers from the 1st Infantry Division, Fort Riley, Kansas deployed during Operation Warm Lakes in support of the Boise Interagency Fire Center (BIFC). The Army soldiers assisted in controlling wildfires in two states in the American West. These two examples highlight the potential diversity of domestic operations that the military might be requested to perform. The most common characteristics of these operations is that they were of limited duration and that federal forces were committed only after they were requested by state governors and/or other civilian agencies. Upon completion of the mission, the military forces concluded operations and in the case of JTF-LA, disbanded. At BIFC, the Fort Riley troops deployed home.

The most significant departure from that norm has been the military's support to the 'War on Drugs'. The DoD's domestic role in the War on Drugs is a current DoD operation, with a standing Joint Task Force (JTF-6) based in El Paso, Texas. Specific statutes within the United States Code (USC) regulate the military support to civilian law enforcement agencies (MSCLEAs) in this and all similar operations.[34] What is important about JTF-6 is its mission, longevity and Area of Operations (AO). The mission of JTF-6 is to, "synchronize operational, training, and intelligence support to domestic law enforcement agencies' counter-drug efforts in the continental United States to reduce the availability of illegal drugs in the United States."[35] The JTF began operations in 1989 with an AO focused primarily along the Southwest U.S. border. In 1995, the JTF's AO expanded to include the entire continental U.S.

The War on Drugs and JTF-6's involvement in it might provide an excellent case study for how the war on terrorism should be fought. The most detailed analysis possible of this comparison is beyond the scope of this monograph. However, a partial examination is offered

---

[33] U.S. Army Field Manual 3-07 (DRAG) *Stability and Support Operations.* 1 Feb 2002 , 6-21.
[34] Title 10 United States Code, Chapter 18 "Military Support to Civilian Law Enforcement Agencies" sections 371-382. Dated 2 January 2001
[35] JTF-6 *Mission Statement.* Internet. Available from http:// www-jtf6.bliss.army mil. Accessed 10 January 2002.

here because the War on Drugs and the War on Terror are quite similar. They both include the

formation of a single national strategy that employs every instrument of national power aimed at

both foreign and domestic audiences. The enemies are global, which includes a large domestic

AO. Due to overlapping AOs, both 'wars' require interagency and joint military operations and

have unique command and control challenges. They also provide an excellent example of how

impediments to progress are reduced, once a threat to the Nation's vital interests is identified.

Finally, the lessons learned from the War on Drugs might save time and effort as the strategy for

Homeland Security and the War on Terror evolves.

Posse Comitatus

In some recent instances, it appears attempts to cite provisions of the Posse Comitatus

Act have become synonymous with the phrase, " that isn't my job" or in the DoD's case, it might

be, " we don't do police work." This Act is often invoked by the DoD as a matter of

convenience, rather than as a matter of necessity. In all fairness to the DoD, the Act has shielded

it from some unusual recent requests.[36] It is also is a federal statute that the DoD must follow, but

one would have to look hard to find anyone in the DoD's leadership lobbying to overturn the Act.

When questioned about the law's relevance and whether it should be refined during Senate

testimony after 11 September, Secretary of the Army Thomas White replied, " I think Senator,

that at this stage, our view is that, in general, the act is fine the way it sits. It reflects a

longstanding tradition of not using federal forces in a law enforcement role that I think serves the

Army well...this longstanding tradition is one that we would like to see prevail."[37] However, in

the post 11 September environment, traditional justifications for mission aversion might not be

appropriate. Therefore, the entire precedent of Posse Comitatus requires a deeper review. If the

---

[36] Soon after 11 September Transportation Secretary Norman Mineta suggested that military personnel, including elite Delta Force special operations troops, be used to provide security on commercial airliners, at least until more air marshals could be trained. "Military Resists Domestic Role" *Government Executive*, Vol. 33, Issue 14 (Nov 2001): 28.
[37] Sec of Army White Senate Testimony 25 Oct 2001.

law is still relevant in today's environment, then it should stay. If not, it needs to go away or be refined. Tradition should not impede security nor should it serve as a bureaucratic roadblock to ensuring that the right assets are applied to the job of Homeland Security. The Act itself is quite simple and concise. It reads:

> Whoever, except in cases and under circumstance expressly authorized by the Constitution of act of Congress, willfully uses any part of the Army or the Air Force as a posse Comitatus or otherwise to execute the laws shall be fined not more than $10,000, or imprisoned not more than two years or both. -18 USC Section 1358-

The history of the Act dates to the period of Reconstruction in the South, following the Civil War. A normal practice in the mid-1800s was for federal marshals and local sheriffs to form a posse in order to assist each other in law enforcement functions. Caleb Cushing, the attorney general to President Franklin Pierce developed a doctrine that authorized marshals and sheriffs to recruit federal soldiers into service as a 'Posse Comitatus' without the assent of the President.[38] The Civil Rights Act of 1866 upheld this practice. During Reconstruction, the military was employed extensively in former confederate States in police roles. The frequency of the military in this role was a cause of concern of many in Congress who felt that, " the Army was becoming politicized and straying away from its original national defense mission."[39] As a result, in 1878, the Congress passed the original version of the Posse Comitatus Act, which ended the use of military forces as a posse to assist federal marshals of sheriffs. There is debate as to the real motive for passing this law. Some feel it was passed to appease confederate states weary of the oppression of Reconstruction policy. Others argue that it was passed to prevent the Army from being used as a national police force; effectively re-focusing the military back to national defense and border protection. Still others felt that it was a practical matter that ended soldiers as

---

[38] Brinkerhoff, John "The Posse Comitatus Act and Homeland Security" *Anser Homeland Security Journal* (Feb 02) Internet. Available from http:// www. homelandsecurity.org/journal/ articles/display Article .asp? article=30 Accessed 1 March 2002.

[39] Trebilcock, Craig "The Myth of Posse Comitatus" (Oct 00) Internet. Available form: http:// www homeland security.org/journal/articles/ displayArticle.asp?article=11 Accessed 20 November 2001.

a posse, as a sort of readily-available, inexpensive police force for locals.[40] Some might say it could have been all the above. Regardless of the exact reason, the law went into effect and subsequently became the most significant legal precedent concerning the use of the military in civilian support actions. It is now a cornerstone ideal of the modern military culture and lexicon.

The Army FMs for Domestic Support Operations (100-19) and the new FM 3-07 (DRAG) Support Operations both include reference to the Posse Comitatus Act. In an attempt to protect commanders, the Army doctrine offers the following précis of 'the law',

> Within the United States, civilian agencies, not the military provide for the needs of citizens. Civilian, federal, state and local government law enforcement agencies execute U.S. laws governing use of the military in domestic support operations are complex, subtle, and ever changing. For this reason, commanders should discuss plans, policies, exercises…with their legal advisors. They should scrutinize each request for aid…to ensure that it conforms with statutory requirements."[41]

The tone of this statement is clearly designed to establish a cognitive division between military members of the DoD, civilian agencies and law enforcement regarding the assignment of roles and definition of operational 'turf'.

In the revised manual FM 3-07 (DRAG) 1 Feb 2002, Stability and Support Operations (not yet official), the doctrine regarding support to civilian law enforcement sends the same message as above:

> It is DoD policy to cooperate with civilian law enforcement officials to the extent practical. However, cooperation must consistently meet the needs of national security and military preparedness, the historic tradition of limiting direct military involvement in civilian law enforcement activities, and the requirements of applicable law.[42]

The authors of this doctrine are not at fault for attempting to protect the DoD and military commanders at all levels from coming in to conflicting with the law. The larger issue here is that in the post 11 September environment there will undoubtedly be changes to existing statutes.

---

[40] Brinkerhoff and Trebilcock articles offer both interpretations.
[41] U.S. Army Field Manual 100-19, *Domestic Support Operations*, July 1993. Pg. 3-1
[42] U.S. Army Field Manual 3-07(DRAG), *Stability and Support Operations*, 1 Feb 02. Pg. 6-18 sec. 6-68.

This can happen rapidly. What does not change quite as rapidly are the attitudes of military professionals who have grown up believing their doctrine.

The final issue addressed here in relation to the Posse Comitatus Act and how it relates to Homeland Security is that for all practical purposes, the Act is not a barrier to using DoD assets in a law enforcement role. In a recent article, Craig Trebilcock writes that the Act is a statutory creation, not a constitutional prohibition. "Accordingly, the Act can and has been repeatedly circumvented by subsequent legislation. Since 1980, the Congress and President have significantly eroded the prohibitions of the Act in order to meet a variety of law enforcement challenges."[43] United States Code Title 10 chapter 18 sections 371-81 are examples of statutory refinements to the Act that resulted from the requirements generated from the War on Drugs.

Summary

Current legal provisions allow the DoD to focus on the 'war fighting' aspects of the anti-terror campaign as their top priority. These arrangements do not require a thorough examination of the intricacies of related domestic law. There are domestic missions and legal complexities that the DoD must eventually address. The current combat air patrols (CAP) are a good example. The Secretary of the Air Force has voiced concern over the high operations tempo (OPTEMPO) involved in this mission and the long-term effects it will have on readiness, which has recently resulted in a scaling back of CAP.[44] In addition to the OPTEMPO concerns are the legal questions raised by having federal forces ordered to shoot down a U.S. civilian airliner perceived to be a threat similar to the planes high-jacked on 11 September.[45] It is difficult to imagine any

---

[43] Trebilcock, 2

[44] Rolfsen, Bruce "Ready or Not, Noble Eagle missions are taxing F-16 pilots so much that 1 in 4 of them may not meet combat qualifications-and they are not alone" *Air Force Times Air Force Times*, 4 March 2002, p.14-18.

[45] Senator Warner, Senate Armed Services Committee, 25 October 2001. pg 8. Discussion concerning Posse Comitatus, and status of belligerent person on US aircraft, requiring authorization to shoot plane down.

other agency within the government of the U.S. conducting this unenviable task. There are many other potential high-level tasks like the CAP mission, which only the DoD can perform.

The principal legal issue at hand is the uncertainty that surrounds commitment of military forces in time of domestic crisis when, "…the boundaries of authority are ambiguous…where defense, law enforcement and protection of civil liberties overlap."[46] When US Air Force jets were patrolling the skies over Washington D.C., prepared to shoot down civilian identified as threats, within ninety minutes of the Pentagon attack, questions of legality were understandably not of immediate concern. In a crisis like that, the President, as Commander-In-Chief, has the authority to use the armed forces to resist attacks against the U.S. This example of executive power is cut and dry. The legal issues become much more complicated within the day-to-day processes of interagency coordination. It is therefore critical that applicable laws are examined and refined as necessary. As one well-known Homeland Security commentator notes, "Inadequate or insufficiently understood legal authorities for a military role in homeland defense against a broad-based WMD challenge pose significant national security risks. They, may for example, delay, complicate, or even prevent defensive measures within …the 50 states and the District of Columbia, measures that would save lives or reduce damage before, during, or after an attack."[47] With this point in mind, it is important that these uncertainties are addressed before the next WMD attack.

Since 11 September, many Congressional leaders have stated that the military must take a more active role in the Homeland Security mission. In the past, U.S. laws and tradition have limited the American military's role in regards to domestic law enforcement activities. These laws and traditions have worked so well that the Nation's predisposition to continue with them cannot be discarded out of hand. These issues are thus important and require a thorough review.

---

[46] Ikle, 16
[47] Ibid., 18.

The relationship between America's military and its citizens is one based on trust, much like the unique relationships between most American citizens and their local law enforcement agencies. However, under current circumstances dictated by 11 September, these traditions must be revisited. It seems probable that the military will take on a more active role in Homeland Security. This must be done without causing an increased 'militarization' of American society.

In conclusion, it is important to note that commitment of federal troops in the U.S. has consistently occurred to protect U.S. citizens, institutions, federal laws and the tenants of the Constitution. The fear that this use of the federal military is inherently a threat to the government is not supported by history or fact. This must be remembered when arguments are made by those who would want to limit military support to civilian authorities by citing a risk to the federal government, especially in the post 11 September world. There has never been an attempted, let alone successful coup in the U.S. This can be attributed to civilian control of the military and the professionalism of the men and women who serve. As the DoD prepares for the possibility of being assigned more domestic missions in support of Homeland Security, it needs to study the lessons learned from past experiences in similar circumstances. An examination of the DoD's role in past Civil Defense activities will provide excellent case studies that closely parallel current Homeland Security issues.

Chapter 2 The Military and Civil Defense

Historical Analysis

Introduction to Civil Defense

The history of Civil Defense in the United States bears a remarkable similarity to the Homeland Security events that are occurring today. By analyzing this history, one can potentially gain a better understanding of some of the realities and challenges of securing the U.S. homeland. Civil Defense is best defined as the organization of the population and governmental support agencies to minimize the effects of enemy action.[48] The earliest attempts to define and institute a federal Civil Defense program were characterized by interagency operations with a heavy lean on the military, especially in times of an increased threat to the continental United States. From a DoD perspective, the history of Civil Defense is typified by poor organization, improper delineation of responsibilities across the entire federal system and a lack of resources.[49] Civil Defense has never clearly fit into the template of defense strategies. It is consistently identified as a key aspect of defense policy yet; it has not always been a defense priority. The episodic nature of Civil Defense in U.S. history is a constant source of internal tension between federal agencies, and an external tension between those same federal entities and the state and local organizations they support.[50] Understanding the source of these tensions and trends of the past is an important step to gaining an appreciation for the difficulty and enormity of developing a Civil Defense or Homeland Security strategy. The first similarity between past attempts at Civil Defense and the current Homeland Security challenge is the commonality of cause.

---

[48] Hopley, Russell J. *Civil Defense for National Security*, pg 1.

[49] DoD is used as a generic term, which includes the War Dept and all defenses, related agencies that now fall under DoD post 1947 NSA.

[50] Naveh, Shimon *In Pursuit of Military Excellence, The Evolution of operational Theory* Tension is cited here in the context of Naveh's construct which states, "Cognitive tension-transpiring from the polarization between the general orientation towards the strategic aim and the adherence to the tactical missions." Pg 13.

Civil Defense in the Inter-War Period

In 1927, General Billy Mitchell warned of the dangers of air attack aimed against the northeast United States industrial centers. He warned, "A few gas, explosive or incendiary shells would force the evacuation of Manhattan for instance."[51] His Douhetian theoretical approach was compelling enough for some people in the War Department to take notice and by 1935; the four U.S. Army area commanders were integrating continental defense measures involving aviation, anti-aircraft artillery, and air warning devices. "Thus, the U.S. Army's first interest in modern Civil Defense grew out of the general concern for over-all continental defense." [52] What it specifically grew out of was a sense of vulnerability by the American military and the American people to an air attack aimed at the homeland. The emergence of longer-range bombers and the sense of insecurity they induced are synonymous to the global terrorist threat faced today.

In 1936, the chief of the Army's Chemical Warfare School took the lead in Civil Defense planning. He issued a pamphlet that stated that the Army had an inescapable responsibility to the civilian population in the area of protection against air attacks.[53] (Keep in mind that the term Army in this setting [Pre 1947 NSA] is almost analogous with the term DoD today.) That same inescapable responsibility for the DoD to defend and secure the U.S. still exists. After September 11, the DoD issued a similar proclamation stating in the Quadrennial Defense Review Report (QDR) released on 30 September 2001, that "the defense of the U.S. Homeland is the highest priority for the U.S. military."[54] Secretary of the Army Thomas White, serving as the interim DoD executive agent for Homeland Security, stated in Senate testimony that: "The QDR…published last month, restores the defense of the United States as the Department's primary mission. Put another way, Homeland Security is job one for the U.S. military-and it has

---

[51] Cooling, Franklin B. "U.S. Army support of Civil Defense: The formative Years" *Military Affairs* Vol. XXXVI No. 1. February 1972. Pg 7.
[52] Ibid., 7.
[53] Ibid., 10.
[54] Department of Defense, *Quadrennial Defense Review Report*. Pg 69.

our full attention."[55] These are somewhat astonishing statements, leaving one to ask, what did the DoD classify as their primary job before 11 September? What these comments clearly illustrate is that once American's feel that the homeland is vulnerable, they look to the DoD for security. It was true in the early days of Civil Defense and it is true now. The post 11 September statements by the DoD were also an attempt to bolster the American public's confidence it their defense establishment and overall security.

World War II Civil Defense

As war emerged on the horizon in both Europe and the Pacific in the late 1930s, Civil Defense issues began to gain momentum. On 18 March 1940, General George Marshall approved the Civil Defense Plan, which laid out several areas that the War Department had responsibility to oversee. The five major tasks assigned to the War Department were: (1) exercise general supervision of Civil Defense planning; (2) provide administrative control of Civil Defense; (3) coordinate Civil Defense with other War Department activities; (4) authorize use of military personnel to assist local, municipal, and state authorities; (5) prepare essential instruction material for the guidance of civil, military and private agencies. In essence, the Civil Defense Plan was the War Departments public acknowledgement that it was the *de facto* lead federal agency for Civil Defense.[56] As WWII progressed it became evident that the War department had to focus on active defense measures and prosecution of a two-theater war, Civil Defense started to become a burden. The heart of the problem was that in times of competing demands and limited resources, both human and physical, priorities had to be established. Just as it is today, it proved difficult to prosecute a war abroad while simultaneously devoting significant effort to protecting the homeland. Several solutions to these challenges emerged. First was the establishment of the

---

[55] Sec of Army White, testimony to Senate Armed Services Committee 25 October 2001.
[56] Cooling, 8.

Office of Civil Defense (OCD) and the interagency Board for Civil Protection. The director of the OCD chaired the interagency meetings, which included members of the Navy, War, and Justice Departments, the Federal Security Agency, the Council of State Governments, the American Municipal Association and the U.S. Conference of Mayors.[57] Additional non-governmental organizations including the Red Cross and the American Legion, the latter becoming the primary trainers of Civil Defense aircraft spotters, also participated in the activities of the board. Second, the War Department attempted to leverage its unique skills and capabilities to train civilian organizations to better cope with the effects of an attack. An example of this was in 1941, the Chemical Warfare services established six regional schools designed to train civilians to handle explosive, incendiary, and gas bombs. Over eight thousand civilian students attended this training and took that knowledge back to their local response organizations. Third, and most importantly during this era, was the acknowledgment by those in both the military and the government that the key to any substantive Civil Defense program was the cooperation between government agencies, be they federal, state or local, and private citizens. This understanding grew out of the realization that Civil Defense was an enormous and extremely complex undertaking. This is also attributed to the recognition that Civil Defense did not only mean protection from an air attack but that it also included developing the systems to effectively manage the consequences of a large scale attack. This is the exact same realization occurring within the federal government and DoD today; that Homeland Defense does not equal Homeland Security.

As the prospect of an Allied victory in World War II grew clearer and the threat of an attack against the continental U.S. diminished the attention given to Civil Defense waned. The fear of an attack was gone, the sense of vulnerability was gone, and the idea of allocating resources towards Civil Defense seemed uneconomical. Thus, in June 1945 the Office of Civil

---

[57] Ibid., 9.

Defense was disbanded. The Civil Defense operations of this era met the requirements but never faced a real test. From a military prospective, the War Department although heavily involved in Civil Defense managed to shed the moniker of lead agency for it. This was a short-lived reprieve for the DoD. As the threat of nuclear war and the vulnerability to attack again emerged during the Cold War, " the Army found itself continuing at the forefront of Civil Defense planning, if more from necessity than ardent desire."[58] Everyone in government acknowledged the importance of Civil Defense but no one wanted to own the task. The Cold War patterns of Civil Defense planning and preparation follow a path similar to the World War II model.

Cold War Civil Defense

The sense of security after the conclusion of World War II did not last long. The Soviet Union's development and testing of nuclear devices forced the Truman administration to address the issue of a federal Civil Defense program. Civil Defense became a key component of the overall defense strategy. Improvements in nuclear devices and delivery means and their potential destructive power threatened the entire framework of the U.S. government. Sustaining the American way of life, protecting the citizens and recovering from an all out nuclear attack were identified as essential tasks of government.

The prevailing attitude in the newly formed DoD was that the key to Civil Defense was 'self help' requiring each level of government to prepare accordingly and that " Civil Defense was not a military responsibility."[59] The DoD under Secretary of Defense James Forrestal leadership did create the office of Civil Defense Planning. This office conducted and prepared a blueprint for future Civil Defense activities.[60] The key recommendation of the report was the

---

[58] Ibid., 11.
[59] Mauck, Elwyn A. "History of Civil Defense in America," *Bulletin of the Atomic Scientists* August-Sept 1950 pg 268-9.
[60] Hopley, Russell J. *Civil Defense for National Security*. An excellent source for detailed outline of Civil Defense organization, purpose, and theory.

creation of a national Civil Defense office. After some reluctance the Truman, administration created the Federal Civil Defense Administration (FCDA).

The central components of the Civil Defense strategy during this era were industrial dispersion, evacuation, and self-protection. Additionally, the FCDA launched extensive public awareness campaigns designed to educate the public.[61] The results of all these efforts were limited. Public apathy plagued the efforts of Civil Defense planners during the early stages of the Cold War.[62] While most citizens acknowledged the threat of a nuclear war but it appears that, they did not feel particularly vulnerable. The proposed costs of adequately preparing for Civil Defense outweighed the perceived threat. The only other significant organizational restructuring during this time came in 1958 with the creation of the Office and Civil Defense Mobilization (OCDM) within the Executive Office of the President.

In the 1960's, President John F. Kennedy attempted to revitalize Civil Defense. After his meeting with Soviet Premier Khrushchev in 1961, and his understanding of the destructive power of the hydrogen bomb Kennedy took steps to protect the population. He clearly understood the ramifications of failure to protect the citizens of the nation and the vulnerable position the country was in. In a televised speech, he stated "To recognize the possibilities of a nuclear war in the missile age without our citizens knowing what they should do and where they should go if bombs begin to fall, would be a failure of responsibility."[63] Kennedy requested and received budget increases to begin ramping up fallout shelter programs. He also directed that the responsibility for Civil Defense move back into The Pentagon (DoD). Once again, in the mind of the President, the DoD was the most logical choice for Civil Defense. In 1964, the Secretary of Defense,

---

[61] In the 1950s the phrase "duck and cover" and the cartoon character Bert the Turtle symbolized Civil Defense public relations and the theme that the one could survive a nuclear exchange if they employed the proper techniques. Noted primarily to appeal to readers old enough to remember the cold war and Civil Defense measures they personally experienced and to highlight commonality of Civil Defense training.
[62] Chipman, William K. *Nonmilitary Defense for The United States, Strategic, Operational, Legal and Constitutional Aspects.* National Securities Studies Group, Madison, WI. 1961: 13-16.
[63] Winkler Alan M., 20.

Robert McNamara transferred the Office of Civil Defense to the Secretary of the Army. In the two years preceding that transfer of responsibility to the Army, the framework of modern military assistance to civilian authorities began to take shape.

In 1962, the discussions surrounding the military's role in Civil Defense centered on the inherent capabilities and priorities of the DoD. Although Civil Defense remained an integral portion of overall defense strategy the DoD continued to lobby for a policy arrangement that placed the lion share of responsibility for Civil Defense upon civilian agencies. The arguments to support the DoD's position were credible. On the surface, the DoD appeared to be the rational choice for Civil Defense operations. The organization, training and equipment capabilities made it an attractive solution for those in government searching for an economical way to provide for Civil Defense. An in depth examination revealed that while the DoD did have unique capabilities it was not the right choice to lead in this endeavor.

The magnitude of a full-scale nuclear exchange would have overwhelmed a Civil Defense program that relied primarily upon DoD. In fact, in the early 1960's the Office of Civil Defense, Department of the Army estimated that, "…if all the military personnel and equipment in the United States were used for Civil Defense, this would represent less than three percent of the Nation's manpower and equipment potential."[64] In addition, the DoD projected that the Soviet's had targeted a large percentage of the forces stationed within continental U.S. An attack upon these forces would have severely hindered their ability to conduct domestic operations. A system built around the military would have created a lack of options if the President wanted to use military forces for combat operations as well as support to civil government.[65] The solution to these problems was the establishment of a DoD task force that studied the problem and then defined the Civil Defense mission parameters. This study resulted in the 1963 Department of

---

[64] Lamson, Robert. "The Army and Civil Defense" *Military Review*, December 1964 pg 8.
[65] Ibid., 8.

Defense Directive, "Military Support to Civil Defense."

The directive outlined the roles and missions that the DoD was willing and capable of executing in support of civil authorities. In summary, the military agreed to prepare for Civil Defense activities and to provide assistance by employing, "available resources that are not required at that time for offensive or defensive operations to assist civil authorities."[66] The new directive was also very clear that Civil Defense was first and foremost a civilian agency responsibility and that the DoD was willing to serve as a compliment to local, state and federal civilian agencies but not as a substitute for them. These general conditions typified the Civil Defense process through the end of the Cold War.

Cold War Civil Defense best illustrates the complexity of preparing large portions of the population for the rigors and hardships of cataclysmic events. During this period, the federal government acknowledged the importance of a fully developed Civil Defense plan and assigned responsibility to the DoD up until 1979. In that year, President Carter ordered that Civil Defense tasks be transferred to the newly established Federal Emergency Management Agency (FEMA). Prior to the transfer, the DoD continued to view its role primarily as a supporting entity to local and state civilian agencies. The result was that Civil Defense was never fully embraced by the DoD, the political leadership or the public. Rather than providing sufficient funding, education and preparation for the public in case of an emergency the federal government opted for the path of least resistance. The old adage, "ignore it and maybe it will go away" seems appropriate when discussing Civil Defense in this era. The same trends continued throughout the last quarter of the twentieth century.

In comparing Cold War and present day activities, the DoD's argument against leading Civil Defense activities during that era was very credible. A Soviet/U.S. full-scale nuclear war represented a threat to the entire structure of American society. That type of conflict would have

---

[66] Ibid., 9.

been a struggle of national survival. Under such circumstances, the DoD would have surely been involved in domestic support operations but the vast amount of its resources would have been engaged in combat missions. Therefore, it was prudent for the DoD to advise that it not be the LFA for Civil Defense. Building a system Civil Defense upon assets that would most likely not exist or dedicated to other higher priority missions would have been irresponsible.

As horrific as the 11 September attacks were, they did not threaten the survival of the U.S.A. The federal government continued to function extremely well. The recovery operations and the current War on Terror are prime examples of that point. The ongoing combat operations have not required the commitment of the entire U.S. military. Proponents of a more active role for the DoD on the domestic front might view this as a window of opportunity to further their agendas.

Post Cold War Civil Defense

Post Cold War federal Civil Defense measures primarily fall under the control of The Federal Emergency Management Agency (FEMA) [67], although the Office of Civil Defense, which was a sub-component of FEMA, was closed in the 1990s. Currently, FEMA is the designated LFA, and assigned the task of consequence management during a domestic WMD attack. The DoD is a designated supporting agency to FEMA in these circumstances. A more in depth explanation of the current system of federal response to a WMD incident will take place in Chapter Three. The important point to note here is that FEMA and not the DoD is the LFA for domestic WMD consequence management. While that is a positive refinement to modern civilian protection measures, much about Civil Defense has changed little in the past fifty years. The questions one must ask themselves is, "What would I do, where would I go, and how do I protect my family in the event of a CBRNE attack in my city?" The fact is most American's cannot

---

[67] National Security Decision Directive NSDD 26, March 26 1982. Designates FEMA as LFA for Civil Defense.

adequately answer that query. This is an area of concern and needs to be addressed by the members of the Office of Homeland Security as they develop a comprehensive strategy.[68]

Summary

Historically, the DoD has consistently lobbied to establish itself as a supporting agency during Civil Defense missions arguing that the task is inherently a civilian function. From the DoD perspective, this is a logical course to pursue. By defining roles and supporting missions before an incident, it allows for the proper allocation and prioritization of resources and training effort. This strategy also allowed the DoD to prioritize and focus on preparations to defend the Nation from the external threats it faces. The fact is however, that the DoD has always been an essential component in domestic operations and continues as such to this day. It is no longer completely feasible to focus the priority of the DoD's efforts and planning on external threats. Now more than ever, it is clear that both internal and external missions relate directly to the security of the Nation. It is no longer realistic to classify threats solely as either foreign or domestic, or Areas of Operation (AO) using that same construct.

On 11 September, the DoD became actively involved in Civil Defense, albeit under the new name of Homeland Security. The preceding analysis has clearly demonstrated that in time of dire circumstances or extreme vulnerability, whether real or perceived, the public looks to the DoD for security.[69] The facts support this essential point. The tension occurs when the DoD dismisses that reality and attempts to divorce itself from the security mission. The new

---

[68] Dobbs, Michael. "A Renaissance for U.S. Civil Defense" Discussion outlining public's lack of readiness for a CBRNE attack.

[69] Feaver, Peter. "The Public's Expectations of National Security*", ...To ensure domestic Tranquility, provide for the common defense ...Papers from the Conference on Homeland Protection.* Strategic Studies Institute. ed. Manwaring, Max G. October 2000. pp 63-5 This article presents findings about the public's attitude concerning the military role in crises. Stating that, "civilians do not think military tools are necessarily more effective than non-military tools: they just think that if the problem is important, we must throw something at it, so we might as well throw the best equipped, best funded tool at our disposal-the military."

operating environment and threat no longer afford this option. Currently, National Guard soldiers provide additional security in most major U.S. airports, Air Force planes patrol the sky over several U.S. cities under the operational control of Commander in Chief NORAD and the Joint Forces Command's (USJFCOM), Joint Task Force Civil Support (JTF-CS) stands ready upon request, to deploy to support civilian authorities in the event of an emergency.[70] The DoD is conducting operations that no one would have imagined before 11 September. Therefore, it is essential that the leadership of the DoD recall the historical precedent concerning the agency's role in Civil Defense. The elected leadership of the Nation equates security with defense. As stated by Senator Carl Levin, Chairman, Committee on Armed Services,

> Those attacks (11 September) have prompted an unprecedented military role in ensuring the security of the United States and the American people. The extraordinary has become the ordinary… These extraordinary responses…require a reexamination of the proper role of the U.S. Armed Forces in helping to ensure the security of the American people[71].

It is important that DoD be involved in the formation of the overarching Homeland Security strategy in order to ensure that assigned missions do not exceed capability and that the DoD meets the perceived expectations of the public in regard to their security.

---

[70] Scott William B. Fighter CAPs Settle into A Routine" Aviation Week and Space Technology. October 22 2001.
[71] Levin, Carl Senator, Chairman Senate Armed Service Committee in Testimony 25 Oct 2001.

Chapter 3 Homeland Security: Background and the Current WMD Response Framework

Presidential Actions

Before the 11 September attacks, the government of the U.S. had taken significant measures to prepare the Nation for such an event. As stated earlier, three terrorist events in the early to middle 1990s served to galvanize support for domestic action. These events were, the 1993 World Trade Center Bombing, the 1995 Murrah Federal Building bombing and the 1995 Tokyo subway system Sarin gas attack. In response to these events and growing evidence concerning WMD proliferation, the federal government took action and laid the groundwork for the system that is currently in place.

On November 14, 1994, President William Clinton issued Executive Order 12938, declaring a national emergency. The order read,

> I, William J. Clinton, President of the United States of America, find that the proliferation of nuclear, biological, and chemical weapons ("weapons of mass destruction") and the means of delivering such weapons, constitutes an unusual and extraordinary threat to the national security, foreign policy, and economy of the United States, and herby declare a national emergency to deal with that threat.[72]

This executive order tasked various departments and agencies with responsibilities for nonproliferation duties and it placed the proper emphasis upon the emerging threats to the Nation. The following is a summary of the most significant Presidential directives concerning protection form terror that followed that declaration of a national emergency:

- Presidential Decision Directive (PDD) 39, U.S. Policy on Counter Terrorism, issued, in June of 1995.[73] PDD 39 represents the impetus for contemporary national terrorism policy. The basic tenets of this directive are grouped into the four following categories: 1) Reducing Vulnerabilities, 2) Deterring Terrorism, 3) Responding to Terrorism, and 4) Weapons

---

[72] Clinton, William J. Executive Order 12938 14 November 1994.
[73] Clinton, William J. Presidential Decision Directive 39. 21 June 1995.

of Mass Destruction. It formalized the LFA, and interagency framework for combating terrorism. The directive also reaffirmed the jurisdictions of LFAs assigning the DOS as the LFA for international terrorism incidents and the DOJ, through the FBI as LFA for terror attacks that occur domestically.

- May of 1998, PDD 62, Combating Terrorism, which "created a new and more systemic approach to fighting the terrorist threat over the next century. It reinforces the missions of the many U.S. agencies charged with roles in defeating terrorism; it also codifies and clarifies their activities in the wide range of U.S. counter-terrorism programs...."[74] Additionally, PDD-62 established the Office of National Coordinator for Security, Infrastructure Protection and Counter-Terrorism. The National coordinator works within the National Security Council and is responsible for overseeing counter-terrorism, protection of critical infrastructure, preparedness and consequence management for WMD policies and programs.

- May of 1998, PDD 63, Critical Infrastructure Protection, which was the result of an infrastructure security study conducted in 1997. This PDD identified the vulnerabilities of both physical infrastructure and cyber-based information systems. The President's intent for this PDD was "that the United States will take all necessary measures to swiftly eliminate any significant vulnerability to both physical and cyber attacks on our critical infrastructures, including especially our cyber systems."[75]

- October 1998, the President signed PDD 67, Enduring Constitutional Government and Continuity of Government Operations. This directive in conjunction with Executive Order 12656 (section 202) are designed to ensure the survival of a constitutional form of government and the continuity of essential federal functions, tasking each federal agency to

---

[74] Office of the Press Secretary, Fact Sheet Combating Terrorism: Presidential Decision Directive 62 May 22 1998. Available on the Internet at http://wwww fas.org/irp/offdocs/pdd-62.htm
[75] Clinton, William J. Presidential Decision Directive 63.Critical Infrastructure, Protection 22 May 1998.

develop a Continuity of Operations Plan (COOP) to ensure that critical elements within the agency could continue too function in time of catastrophe.[76]

- October 2001, President G.W. Bush signed and issued two Homeland Security Presidential Directives (HSPD). The first established the Homeland Security Council and Homeland Security Council Principles Committee (HSC/PC)[77] The second HSPD outlines the methodology to combat terrorism through immigration policies. In March of 2002 a third HSPD was issued which established the Homeland Security Advisory System.

Stafford Act

In 1984, the United States Congress passed the Robert T. Stafford Disaster Relief Act. The law authorizes the commitment of federal military forces upon request, and under the control of the FEMA (or designated LFA), in order to mitigate damage caused by natural disaster or emergency. The Act also authorized the development of the Federal Response Plan (FRP), which enumerates interagency and departmental responsibilities in time of emergency. Under the FRP, applicable federal agencies are each assigned Emergency Support Functions (ESF). The DoD has primary responsibility for ESF number 3, Public Works and Engineering, and has supporting responsibilities in the remaining eleven ESFs.[78] An example of forces committed under the provisions of the Stafford Act is the 1992 deployment of elements of the 18th Airborne Corps to Florida. The federal forces organized as a JTF and provided relief form Hurricane Andrew in Southern Florida. The JTF executed missions in conjunction with local, State, federal and private organizations.[79] In order to incorporate the provisions of this act, and in light of its role in

---

[76] Clinton, William J PDD-NSC-67 Enduring Constitutional Government and Continuity of Government Operations. 21 October 1998

[77] Bush, George W. "Homeland Security Presidential Directive-1, Organization and Operation of the Homeland Security Council." Internet. Available from at:http://www fas.org/irp/offdocs/nspd/hspd-1.htm

[78] FEMA, Federal Response Plan (FRP) Internet. Available from http://www fema.gov/r-n-r/frp/. Accessed 10 Jan 2002.

[79] Lujan, Thomas R. "Legal Aspects of Domestic Employment of the Army," *Parameters*, XXVII, no. 3 (Autumn 1997): 82-97.

disaster relief the DoD designated the U.S. Army as the Executive Agent for Domestic Support Operations. It also created the Director of Military Support (DOMS) within the office of the Secretary of the Army to serve as liaison during commitment of federal forces to civilian assistance missions and domestic preparedness training.

The Defense Against Weapons of Mass Destruction Act

In 1996, the Congress mandated that the DoD provide WMD training and assistance to local and state civilian agencies to better prepare first responders for the challenges of a WMD incident. The legal justification came from the passage of The Defense Against Weapons of Mass Destruction Act, which directed the establishment of the Nunn-Lugar-Domenici (NLD) domestic preparedness program.[80] The goal of the NLD domestic preparedness program was to, " enhance federal, state, and local emergency response capabilities to deal with a domestic terrorist incident involving WMD.[81] By law, the DoD was designated the LFA for implementation of the NLD program. As lead agency, DoD was responsible for interagency coordination and the training of response teams in the Nation's 120 largest cities. The assignment of lead agency to the DoD in the above example is clear evidence that as the threat of domestic terror increases so does the DoD's involvement in combating it. Additionally, it is evidence that the Congress of the U.S. is not adverse to tapping into the unique resources of the DoD if they perceive a viable threat exists. Although LFA status for NLD provisions transferred from DoD to DOJ, in October 2001, the DoD did provide and conduct WMD training in almost half of the identified 120 cities. The Army's Soldier Biological Chemical Command (SBCCOM) was the principle agency that executed this training.[82] These two acts by the Congress, passed long before the 11 September attacks, further solidified the relations between the DoD and civilian authorities and agencies. The 1984 Stafford Act was established to allow the use of federal military through FEMA to

---

[80] United States General Accounting Office, *Combating Terrorism, Threat and Risk Assessment Can Help Prioritize and Target Program Investments*, Washington, D.C.: 1998. Pg 2.
[81] Ibid., 1.

support state and local civilian governments in order to mitigate pain, suffering, and lose of property during a disaster. The 1996 Act, as the threat of WMD incidents increased, attempted to leverage DoD's unique capabilities and resources in dealing with the complex and chemical, biological and nuclear threat.

Each of the above-described directives, orders and Acts were the result of the identification of a void in civilian capability, increased threat awareness, and the recognition of existing vulnerabilities within American society. These mandates illustrate that the federal government has clearly identified its responsibility to provide assistance in time of catastrophe, be they man made or natural. They also illustrate that much had been done to prepare the U.S. before 11 September. This point is often overlooked as people clamor for wholesale reconfiguration of the Nation's current security system.

DoD and Domestic WMD The Current Framework

The current operational framework for the federal government's response to a WMD incident is more capable then one might be inclined to believe. The DOJ and the FEMA have developed base plans that adhere to the Presidential guidance and address emerging threats. In the field of consequence management, the DoD appears to be poised to meet its supporting agency requirements.[83] In the post 11 September environment, the potential magnitude and scope of a single or worse, simultaneous WMD attacks, has required most federal agencies to reassess their current plans and capabilities. This does not mean that the work done to this point was inadequate. On the contrary, while much work still needs to be done, the system in place is feasible, and provides a workable start point for expansion.

---

[82] Larson and Peters, 72.

[83] FEMA, in Coordination with the Catastrophic Disaster Response Group "An Assessment of Federal Consequence Management Capabilities For Response to Nuclear, Biological, or Chemical (NBC) Terrorism, A Report to the President" This report concluded that when augmented by specialized units, the FRP was readily adaptable for NBC terrorism response, while a bit dated, this report supports the idea that the current systems are adaptable and capable, and that the LFA roles are adequate.

In the current federal response system, the commitment of federal assets occurs only after the appropriate local and state officials request it. In the majority of WMD incident scenarios, local and state emergency officials will be the first on the scene, the aptly called 'first responders'. This realization provided the impetus for the 1996 NLD legislation. It also led to the creation of mobile federal response capabilities designed to bolster and supplement local resources. Within the current system, the DoD is not assigned LFA responsibility for either consequence or crisis management tasks, but the department does have a significant supporting role.

The United States Government Interagency Domestic Terrorism Concept of Operations Plan is one of the primary documents that outline interagency commitments and departmental responsibilities during a domestic WMD terrorist incident.[84] Signatories to this document include the following: the Secretaries of Defense, Energy, Health and Human Services, the Directors of the FBI and FEMA, the Administrator of the Environmental Protection Agency (EPA) and the Attorney General. A summary of DoD's role within this document follows,

> DoD serves as a support agency to the FBI for crisis management functions, including technical operations, and a support agency to FEMA for consequence management. In accordance with DoD directives 3025.15 and 2000.12 and the CJCS CONPLAN 0300-97, and upon approval by the secretary of Defense, DoD will provide assistance to the LFA and or the CONPLAN primary agencies, as appropriate, during all aspects of a terrorist incident, including both crisis and consequence management. DoD assistance includes threat assessment; Domestic Emergency Support Team (DEST) participation and transportation; technical advice; operational support; tactical support; support for civil disturbances; custody, transportation and disposal of a WMD device; and other capabilities including mitigation of the consequences of a release. The DoD has many unique capabilities for dealing with WMD, such as the US Army Medical Research Institute for Infectious Diseases, Technical Escort Unit (TEU) and USMC Chemical Biological Incident response force. These and other DoD assets may be used in responding to a terrorist incident if requested by the LFA and approved by the Secretary of Defense[85].

---

[84] FEMA, *United States Government Interagency Domestic Terrorism Concept of Operations Plan*. Internet. Available from http://www.fema.gov/r-n-r/conplan.pdf; Accessed 26 January 2002.
[85] Ibid., 4.

The DoD has organized itself to handle the above assigned tasks in an efficient manner. At strategic level, the following steps have been taken: creation of the Office of Assistant to the Secretary of Defense for Civil Support; delegation of responsibility to the US Army to serve as the DoD Executive Agent for Military Assistance to Civil Authorities (MACA); the formation of the Director of Military Support (DOMS) office; and the recent designation of the Secretary of the Army as the DoD interim Executive Agent for Homeland Security. At the Operational level, the DoD has effectively developed WMD response capabilities[86]. (It is important note that the DoD is only one of eight federal agencies that have twenty-four types of teams that have a CBRNE incident response capability.[87]) The DoD actively participates in interagency training exercises and provides support to both LFA's in accordance with pre-existing agreements.[88] Additionally, DoD has established two standing JTFs to address possible terrorist activity. Joint Task Force Computer Network Defense (JTF-CND) is a sub-element of SPACECOM and DoD centric. This JTF has the responsibility to develop strategies to protect DoD computer networks. The second is Joint Task Force Civil Support (JTF-CS). This JTF, established in 1999, is a component of USJFCOM with the mission of deploying to a WMD incident site and establishing a command and control headquarters to facilitate and control all federal military assets that respond. A very interesting point to make a note of is that this JTF did not deploy any assets to New York City in support of the 11 September terrorist attacks.[89] This exemplifies the high level of preparedness of New York City's first responders, city government, and the New York National Guard. The non-involvement of JTF-CS was also attributed to the geographic isolation

---

[86] U.S. General Accounting Office Report to Congressional Requesters *Combating Terrorism Federal Agencies Efforts to Implement National Policy and Strategy* GAO/NSIAD-97-254 Appendix III pg 79. This appendix lists each federal agency capabilities to support a WMD incident. DoD specific include TEUs, EOD, USMC Chemical Biological incident response Force Army CRTs, US Naval Medical research institute, and the army medical research institute.
[87] Ibid., 4. Additional federal agencies with CBRNE response capability are: DOE, HHS, Transportation, VA, FEMA, EPA, and the NRC.
[88] US DOJ, Office of Justice Programs, Office for Domestic Preparedness (ODP) "Exercise Planning and Support, from the Office for Domestic Preparedness Support" Internet. Available from: www.ojp.usdoj.gov/odp/ta/overview htm Accessed 15 March 2002.

of the attack. Concerning doctrine, the Joint Publications 3-07 Joint Doctrine for MOOTW, and 3-08 Interagency Coordination During Joint Operations volumes I and II appear to adequately address the overarching principles of providing support to civilian authorities in the interagency environment. They serve as an adequate guide for the Services to develop their own specific doctrinal manuals.

Summary

Substantial effort in the past has laid the groundwork for an effective response to WMD incident. The DoD appears prepared to meet its current Consequence Management mission requirements for a domestic WMD attack under the current provisions, laws and agreements. This does not mean that the current federal system will not undergo significant changes in the future but it does mean that the outlook is not as bleak as earlier thought. A recent GAO report suggested that the wide variety of federal response capability provides flexibility in determining which specialized assets should be committed in case of attack. The same report also concluded that a key to increased effectiveness is national level training sponsored by FEMA and the DOJ.[90] Through continued training and exercises, identified shortcomings can be fixed resulting in increased effectiveness. There is no cause to overhaul the entire domestic WMD consequence management response structure or the DoD's assigned tasks. The key components of the existing system include temporary DoD assistance and a primarily supporting agency role. The argument to increase the DoD's role in crisis management is more complicated.

Several of the tasks associated with crisis management appear to conflict with the long-standing traditions of the role of the military in civil society, primarily in the area of law enforcement activities. As mentioned earlier, the provisions of Posse Comitatus prevent military

---

[89]Telephone Interview conducted by author with Col Routen Deputy Commander JTF-CS 12 March 2002.
[90] Report to Congressional Requesters *Combatting Terrorism Federal Response Teams Provide Varied Capabilities; Opportunities remain to Improve Coordination* pg 4-25. Report highlights DOJ and FEMA sponsored exercise TOPOFF 2000, which occurred in May 2000 simulated no notice WMD attacks in New Hampshire, Washington D.C. and a biological incident in Denver Colorado.

forces from engaging in law enforcement unless ordered to do so by the President or under the specific refinements to current federal statute (as with the 'War on Drugs'). The DoD is not in a position to reform legislation. The solution seems to be that The Congress must study the issue and refine the law if it is in the best interest of the Nation. It is likely that, just as in the War on Drugs the perceived threat warrants change. This could potentially equal an increase in mission responsibility and tasking for the DoD.

Chapter 4 Conclusions and Recommendations

Conclusion

Before 11 September 2001, there were many 'how to' suggestions and theories for conducting, organizing and executing Homeland Security.[91] The emerging threats of an enemy employing asymmetrical means and WMD to avoid U.S. strengths and attack the Nation's vulnerabilities had been well documented. The Hart-Rudman Commission in 2001, and public comments made by President Clinton and other executive branch leaders clearly show that there was indeed an understanding that the U.S. was likely to endure some type of WMD terrorist attack early in the twenty-first century.[92] Some of the common recommendations had included: development of a comprehensive National Homeland Security Strategy, creation of a new federal executive level position that dealt only with Homeland Security issues, creation of a new regional Commander-in Chief (CINC) within the DoD, and reorganization of some of the current interagency relationships regarding Homeland Security.

Within a month after the 11 September attack, President Bush established the Homeland Security Council and the Office of Homeland Security, naming Governor Tom Ridge as its head. This office is currently responsible for developing a National Homeland Security Strategy, and Governor Ridge is now the Executive Assistant to the President for Homeland Security. The DoD has recommend the creation of a new regional Commander in Chief (CINC), most likely

---

[91] Kelly, Terrence. "An Organizational Framework for Homeland Defense," *Parameters*, XXXI, no. 3, (Autumn 2001):105-116. US Commission on National Security/21st Century, Road Map for National Security: *"Imperative for Change, The Phase III Report"* pg 14-7. Dobbs, Michael "Homeland Security: New Challenges for an Old Responsibility" All three in part recommended establishment of a Homeland security agency, a single national coordinator, and LTC Kelly advocated a CINC for the homeland.

[92] Larsen and Peters,16-17. Leadership Statements. Quotes from President Clinton and Richard Clarke stating their concerns about identified WMD vulnerabilities in the U.S.

called Northern Command (NORTHCOM), with an Area Of Operations (AO) that would include the Continental U.S.[93]

The primary task of NORCOM will be Homeland Security.[94] For all practical purposes, it appears that of the four common recommendations concerning Homeland Security before 11 September, three are now in the works and the fourth is inevitable. However, the key, critical issues to guarantee Homeland Security are still a long way from being resolved.

In one respect what might be at issue, is the role of the DoD within American society. Through the course of this monograph, an attempt has been made to describe some of the factors that ultimately define what the DoD is and does, as an instrument of the government and servant of the people and how those roles have evolved throughout the history of the Nation. In the discussion concerning legal considerations of the DoD's role, the historical precedence that exists is one that values civilian control of the military and the limited use of federal forces in civilian law-enforcement activities. However, it also clearly illustrated that in time of need, the federal military can and will be employed domestically to secure the interests of the Nation. The discussion of Civil Defense proves that when the Nation has felt vulnerable, both the public and elected officials have immediately looked to the DoD for security.

The common thread that appeared in the first two chapters of this monograph was that the DoD appeared somewhat reluctant to execute missions that brought it into conflict with domestic law, or with its perceived primary mission orientation. Yet, in almost every case, the perceived consequence of DoD involvement to the interests of the Nation overrode the lines that separated the DoD from tasks it did not want to perform. Based on these historical examples, the DoD can

---

[93]"Rumsfeld Envisions New Command responsible for Homeland Security." *Inside the Pentagon*, 17 January, 2002. Internet. Available from: http://ebird.dtic.mil/Jan2002/e20020117envisions htm Accessed 20 January 2002.

[94] McLaughlin, Abraham "Pentagon Homeland Role: Office In Search of a Mission," *Christian Science Monitor* February 25 2002. Internet. Available from:http://ebird.dtic mil/Feb2002/e20020225 pentagon htm . Accessed 1 March 2002. Article quotes CJCS General Myers stating the three primary missions for NORCOM.

presume that in times of crisis, changes to its primary missions are inevitable. Therefore, it is important to forecast those shifts, and to get ahead of change in order to limit the use of 'ad hoc' fixes at critical times. This analysis strongly supports the idea that the DoD establishes a new Homeland CINC. The third chapter outlined the current framework under which the DoD supports LFAs in a WMD incident. Contrary to the beliefs of some, the DoD is today heavily engaged in WMD Consequence Management response activities. Furthermore, the current system provides a workable solution and feasible starting points for necessary change.

It is also very important to note that the concepts and policies surrounding Homeland Security and a National Homeland Security Strategy continue to evolve in the months following 11 September. To date, there still does not exist a comprehensive, overarching national plan that covers all aspects of Homeland Security. As the current structure of the Nation's security framework is continuously reviewed in light of new and emerging threats, the DoD has an obligation to keep an open mind.

There appears to be a struggle on the horizon between the DoD and the political leadership of the Nation as the Department's future roles are defined. If it happens, at the center of this fight will be the OHS. As the comprehensive strategy for Homeland Security takes form, there are undoubtedly going to be increased demands on the DoD to fulfill a larger, more active role. The primary arguments of those supporting this change will include the fact that no other agency can execute some of the new Homeland Security tasks as easily as the DoD. Given that they have significant latitude as they develop new strategy, OHS would be wise to build requirements based on the effects they desire, not on the capability they think they need. In many cases, this will cause a default of tasks to the DoD. For example, no other agency can secure the airspace over the continental U.S. Nor is there another agency with the inherent capability to rapidly mobilize large numbers of people and specialized equipment on the scale required to respond to a major WMD attack.[95] Both of these capabilities are key components of an overall Homeland Security Strategy.

Perhaps Secretary of Defense Rumsfeld was technically correct when he stated that it was not the DoD's responsibility to have prevented the events of 11 September 2001. However, in the same breath, he also stated that the current 'arrangements' required review. This monograph has provided an initial review of the requirements of the DoD in Homeland Security, with an eye towards meeting the changing needs and expectations of the Nation. By understanding the expectations of the public in post 11 September America, the existing domestic commitments of the DoD, as well as the historical use of the DoD in Homeland Security-type missions and the realities of the current threat of WMD attacks, one is much better prepared to meet the challenges of the new security environment.

Recommendations

The first two recommendations address the refinement of current doctrine and are quite simple. The terms 'Homeland Security' and 'Homeland Defense' must be clearly defined and included in Joint Doctrine, specifically in JP-1.02 Department of Defense Dictionary of Military and Associated Terms. This will provide a firm base from which the services can develop their own service-specific doctrine on this subject. In addition, the US Army needs to refine the language in both FM 100-19 Domestic Support Operations, and FM 3-07 (DRAG) Stability and Support Operations, specifically concerning the Army's relations with and responsibilities to, civilian agencies. The current text in these publications does not portray the correct interagency themes required in the post 11 September environment.

The second recommendation is the creation of new regional/functional Commander-in-Chief (CINC) with a primary Area of Responsibility (AOR) of the Continental U.S., but that also

---

[95]Hamre, John J. "A Strategic Perspective On US Homeland Defense: Problem and Response" in "...*To ensure domestic Tranquility, provide for the common defense ...*" ed. Manwaring, Max, 11-25

includes a global planning responsibility (CINCNORCOM). (While it appears creation of this new HQ is a forgone conclusion, this recommendation is concerned with the structure, mission and AO of this new headquarters.) This recommendation is based on the conclusions of the historical analysis presented earlier throughout this monograph. In times of crisis or threat, the expectations of U.S. citizens and their elected representatives is one that consistently places the responsibility for securing the Nation upon the DoD. Therefore, to properly meet these expectations, the time to plan and prepare for Homeland Security is now, in order to avoid on the fly fixes. By creating the CINCNORCOM position and headquarters, the DoD will have a single organization that is poised to focus solely on the mission of Homeland Security.

Currently, USJFCOM is the responsible entity for Homeland Security. One need only to read the USJFCOM mission statement to understand that this organization is not, in its current form, the right headquarters to focus on Homeland Security. [96] The new CINCNORCOM, in addition to the being responsible for domestic Homeland Security should also be responsible for developing and coordinating the overarching global military campaign against terrorism. This would allow for a single campaign plan that transcends the geographic divisions that currently exist among CINCs AORs. The function of this headquarters would coincide nicely with the proposed definition of Homeland Security offered in the introduction of this monograph. The task of coordinating the efforts against terror across the current Goldwater-Nichols framework will not be easy. However, the global, as well as the interagency nature of this conflict renders the current geographic divisions among AORs antiquated and ineffective. Consider the potential lessons lost and opportunities missed if the War on Terror moves sequentially from Central

---

[96] USJFCOM mission statement reads, " As chief advocate for jointness, USJFCOM maximizes the nation's future and present military capabilities through joint concept development and experimentation, recommending joint requirements, advancing interoperability, conducting joint training and providing ready continental U.S. based forces and capabilities to support other combatant commanders-in-chief, the Atlantic Theater and domestic requirements." The CINC USJFCOM is also the Supreme Allied Commander, Atlantic (SACLANT). All tasks assigned to USJFCOM are important, however it appears that the assignment of CINC homeland security might over task this organization.

Command (CENTCOM) to Pacific Command (PACOM), or the operational confusion as the war is executed in two AORs simultaneously. One headquarters with the responsibility of planning, coordinating and overseeing the execution of the global effort is required.

Structurally, NORTHCOM should absorb JTF-6, JTF-CS, JTF-CND, as well as NORAD. The HQ must also include some type of office (perhaps a refined JTF-CND) that interfaces, trains and assists private sector corporations that are vulnerable to cyber attack. Additionally, NORCOM should be charged with developing and leading interagency training exercises that encompass every aspect of Homeland Security operations.[97] The relationship between NORCOM, DOJ, FEMA and the OHS are undoubtedly going to be extremely complex. The salient point is that unity of effort cannot be diluted by interagency rivalry and misunderstanding.

It is also recommended that the DoD does not inherit the title of LFA for Homeland Security. The current Consequence and Crisis Management systems and interagency support relationships are adequate. The creation of a new CINC headquarters will facilitate DoD's ability to prioritize the sensitive domestic issues involving Homeland Security, while easing the burden on USJFCOM. It will also centralize the planning and execution of the global War on Terror.

The final recommendation concerns the mental and institutional approach the DoD takes in regard to Homeland Security. In an earlier portion of this monograph, an example was cited that recounted a request by Secretary of Transportation, Norman Mineta, asking the DoD for Special Forces soldiers to serve as interim air marshals on domestic airline flights shortly after 11 September. At first glance, this appears to be a ludicrous request. From a different perspective, it might not have been so unreasonable. If another incident similar to 11 September occurs and DoD asset that might have potentially averted the incident sit idle, denied use because the requested task does not make the list of things that the DoD is willing to do, then the DoD has

---

[97] Campbell, Kurt M. Flournoy, Michele A. *To Prevail, An American Strategy For The Campaign Against Terrorism.* Washington D.C.: CSIS, 2001, 335-6.

ultimately failed to meet its security obligations. In the post 11 September environment, some interim fixes and untraditional approaches are in order, while other less robust agencies build their capability. While patrolling the border or guarding critical infrastructure facilities are not missions that the DoD is currently accustomed to doing, in the short term they might be required. Just as portions of the new anti-terrorism legislation include 'sun-set' clauses so too can some of the DoD's interim tasks for Homeland Security.

It is critical that every effort is made to ensure that a balance exists between the DoD and the many other federal agencies that are involved in Homeland Security. The DoD must be willing to accept untraditional missions in the new environment. Historically, the public does not categorize threats in a foreign or domestic construct. Therefore, the DoD must embrace its role in domestic operations while balancing it with the global War on Terror.

Bibliography

Barnes, Joseph R. "Despite The Posse Comitatus Act, Are Federal Soldiers About to Deploy as Deputized Border Patrol Customs Agents?" (February 2002): *ANSER Journal of Homeland Security*, Internet. Available form: http:// www. homelandsecurity.org/ journal/Commentary/ displayCommentary.asp?commentary=11. Accessed 3 March 2002.

Brinkerhoff, John R. "The Posse Comitatus Act and Homeland Security," (February 2002): *ANSER Journal of Homeland Security*, Internet. Available form: http:// www. homelandsecurity.org/journal/articles/ displayArticle.asp?article=30 Accessed 1 March 2002.

Campbell, Kurt, and Flournoy, Michele. *To Prevail An American Strategy for the Campaign Against Terrorism.* Washington D.C.: CSIS Press, 2001.

Chaisson, Kernan A. 2001. "NSGG Homeland Defense Recommendations." *Journal of Electronic Defense* 24 no. 4 (April): 18.

Chipman, William K. *Nonmilitary Defense for the United States, Strategic, Operational, legal and Constitutional Aspects.* Madison Wisconsin: National Security Studies Group Press, 1961.

Cooling, Franklin B. "US Army Support of Civil Defense: The Formative Years," *Military Affairs*, XXXV, no. 1 (February 1971): 7-10.

_____. "Civil Defense and the Army: The Quest for Responsibility," *Military Affairs*, XXXVI, no. 1 (February 1972): 11-13.

Cooper Jerry M. "Federal Military Intervention," in *The United States Military Under the Constitution of the United States*, 1789-1989. ed. Kohn, Richard, 123-36. New York: New York University Press, 1991

Cordesman, Anthony H. "Defending America: Redefining the Conceptual Borders of Homeland Defense," Washington D.C. Center for Strategic and International Studies, 2000.

Dickinson, Lansing E. "The military Role in Countering Terrorist Use of Weapons of Mass Destruction," *Counter-proliferation Papers, Future Warfare Series*, no. 1, USAF Counter-proliferation Center, Air War College, September 1999.

Dobbs, Michael. "Homeland Security: New Challenges for an Old Responsibility," (March 2001)*: ANSER Journal of Homeland Security*, Internet. Available form: http:// www. homelandsecurity. org/journal/articles/ displayArticle.asp?article=4 Accessed 30 December 2001.

_____. "A Renaissance for U.S. Civil Defense?" (July 2001): *ANSER Journal of Homeland Security*, Internet. Available form: http:// www. homelandsecurity. org/journal/articles/ displayArticle.asp?article=7 Accessed 30 December 2001.

_____. "Establishing a CINC for Homeland Security," (October 2001): *ANSER Journal of Homeland Security*, Internet. Available form: http:// www. homelandsecurity. org/journal/articles/ displayArticle.asp?article=22 Accessed 30 December 2001.

Domenici, Pete V. "Countering Weapons of Mass Destruction," *The Washington Quarterly* 18, no. 1 (Winter 1995): 145-52.

Erickson, Richard J. *Legitimate Use of Military Force Against State Sponsored International Terrorism.* Maxwell Air Force Base: Air University Press, 1989.

Farrell, William Regis. *The U.S. Government Response to Terrorism: In Search of an Effective Strategy*, Boulder Colorado: Westview Press, 1982.

Foster, Gaines M. *The Demands of Humanity: Army Medical Disaster Relief.* Washington D.C.: U.S. Government Printing Office, 1983.

Grange, David and Johnson, Rodney. "Forgotten Mission: Military Support to the Nation, " *Joint Forces Quarterly*, (Spring 1997): 108-15.

Hamilton, Alexander, Jay John and Madison, James. *The Federalist Papers. With an Introduction by Gary Willis.* New York: Bantam Books, 1982.

Hopley, Russell J. (Director*) Civil Defense for National Security.* Office of Civil Defense Planning, Washington D.C.: U.S. Government Printing Office, 1949.

Ikle, Fred C. "Defending the U.S. Homeland Strategic and Legal Issues for DOD and the Armed Services," *CSIS Homeland Defense Working Group* January 1999

Kelly, Terrence. "An Organizational Framework for Homeland Defense," *Parameters*, Vol XXXI, no. 3 (Autumn 2001) : 105-16.

Kerr, James W. "Organization for Civil Defense," *Military Review* XLVIII, no. 3 (March 1968): 75-82.

Kohn, Richard, ed. *The United States Military Under the Constitution of the United States, 1789-1989*. New York: New York University Press, 1991.

Lake, Anthony. *6 Nightmares.* New York: Little Brown and Company, 2000.

Lamson, Robert. "The Army and Civil Defense," *Military Review*, XLIV, no. 12 (December 1964): 3-12.

Larson, Eric V. and Peters, John E. *Preparing the U.S. Army for Homeland Security Concepts, Issues, and Options*, Santa Monica, CA: Rand Publishing, 2001.

Lawlor, Bruce M (Commander JTF-CS) "Military Support of Civilian Authorities A New Focus For a New Millennium," (October 2000, updated September 2001): *ANSER Journal of Homeland Security*, Internet. Available form: http:// www. homelandsecurity.org/ journal/articles/ displayArticle.asp?article=10. Accessed 10 January 2002.

Lujan, Thomas R. "Legal Aspects of Domestic Employment of the Army," *Parameters*,. XXVII, no. 3 (Autumn 1997): 82-97.

Manwaring, Max, ed. *...to insure domestic Tranquility, provide for the common defence... .* Carlisle, Pennsylvania: Strategic Studies Institute Press, 2000.

Manwaring, Max and Olson, WM J. ed. *Managing Contemporary Conflict, Pillars of Success.* Boulder: Westview Press, 1996.

McDermott, Edward A. "Emergency Planning," *Military Review*, XLIV, no. 2 (February 1964): 19-28.

McLaughlin, Abraham "Pentagon Homeland Role: Office In Search of a Mission" *Christian Science Monitor* February 25 2002

McGuckin, Frank, ed. *Terrorism in the United States. Vol. 69 number 1, The Reference Shelf.* New York: The H.W. Wilson Company, 1997.

Metz, Steven, "Asymmetric Warfare: Strategic Asymmetry." *Military Review* 81 (Jul/Aug 2001):22-31.

Moore, Michele Marie. *Oklahoma City Day One.* Eagar: The Harvest Trust, 1997.

Naveh, Shimon *In Pursuit of Military Excellence The Evolution of Operational Theory*, London: Frank Cass Publishing, 1997.

Pelletiere, Stephen C., ed. *Terrorism: National Security Policy and the Home Front.* Carlisle: US Army War College, SSI, 1995.

Perret, Geoffrey. *Old Soldiers Never Die The Life of Douglas MacArthur.* Holbrook: Adams Media Corporation, 1997.

Roxborough, Ian. *The Hart-Rudmann Commission and the Homeland Defense.* Carlisle: US Army War College, SSI, 2001.

Schweitzer, Glenn, and Dorsch Carole. *Superterrorism, Assassins, Mobsters, and Weapons of Mass Destruction.* New York: Plenum Trade, 1998.

Scott, William B. "Fighter CAPs Settle Into A routine," *Aviation Week and Space Technology.* (22 October 2001): 76-7.

Seigrist, David and Graham, Janice. *Countering Biological Terrorism in the US: An Understanding of Issues and Status.* Vol. 4, Second Series, *Terrorism: Documents of International and Local Control* by Alexander, Yonah and Musch, Donald. New York: Oceana Publications, 1999.

Shaughnessy, David and Cowan, Thomas "Attack on America: The First War of the 21st Century" *Military Review* 83 (November-December 2001). Internet. Available from: http://www-cgsc.army.mil/milrev/English/Nov-Dec/shaugh.htm Accessed 15 February 2002.

Snider, Don M, and Carew, Miranda, eds. *U.S. Civil-Military relations, In Crisis or Transition?* Washington D.C.: CSIS, 1995.

Stanton, John J., "U.S. Homeland Defense Policy Mired in Competing Interests," *National Defense* 85 no.567 (Feb 2001): 10-13.

Stringer, Kevin, " A Homeland Defense Mission." *Military Review* 80 no.3 (May/June 2000): 98-101.

Stuart, Douglas, ed. *Organizing for National Security*. Carlisle: US Army War College, SSI, 2000.

Taylor, Max and Horgan John. Ed. *The Future Of Terrorism.* London: Cass Publishers, 2000.

Thornberry, Mac, and Taylor, Eric, "Symposium: Q: Is a New Federal Agency Needed to Defend Against Terrorist Attacks?," *Insight on the News* 17 no. 12 (Mar 2001): 40-43.

Trebilcock, Craig T. "Posse Comitatus-Has the Posse Outlived its Purpose?," (October 2000): *ANSER Journal of Homeland Security*, Internet. Available form: http:// www. homelandsecurity.org/journal/articles/ displayArticle.asp?article=11 Accessed 20 November 2001.

Treverton, Gregory F "Covert Action and Open Society," *Foreign Affairs* 65, no. 5 (Summer 1987): 995-1014.

Turabian, Kate L. *A Manual for Writers of Term Papers, Theses, and Dissertations*. 6th ed. Chicago: University of Chicago Press, 1996.

U.S. Congress. Senate. Armed Services Committee. "U.S. Senate Armed Services Committee Holds Hearing On the Department of Defense's Role In Homeland Security," *FDCH Political Transcripts*, 25 October 2001. Internet. Available from http:// ehostvgw7.epnet.com/fulltext., Accessed 17 December 2001

U.S. Code. Title 10, Armed Forces, Chapter 18, Military Support for Civilian Law Enforcement Agencies sec.. 371-382.

U.S. Constitution, art I, sec. 8.

U.S. Constitution, Preamble.

U.S. Constitution, art IV sec. 4.

US Joint Forces Command, *Mission Statement and Organization* Internet. Available from: http:// 137.246.33.101About/about/htm. Accessed 27 Feb 2002.

_____. Joint Task Force Civil Support, *Mission Statement and Organization* Internet. Available from: http:// 137.246.33.101About/com_jtfcs.htm. Accessed 27 Feb 2002.

_____. Joint Task Force 6, *Mission Statement*. Internet. Available from http:// www-jtf6.bliss.army.mil. Accessed 10 January 2002.

Weiss, Aaron. "When Terror Strikes Who Should Respond?" *Parameters* Vol XXXI, no. 3 (Autumn 2001): 117-31.

Wilkinson, Paul. *Terrorism and the Liberal State*. New York: John Wiley and Sons, 1977.

Wing, Ian. "Refocusing Concepts of Security, The Convergence of Military and Non-military Tasks," *Working Paper 111*, Land Warfare Studies Center, November 2000.

Winkler, Alan M. "A 40-year History Of Civil Defense," Bulletin of the Atomic Scientist, 40, no. 6 (June –July 1984): 16-23.

Newspaper Articles

Gray, Jerry. "Senate Approves Anti-Terror Bill By A 91-to-8 Vote, Bombings Were Catalyst," *New York Times*, 8 June 1995, sec A1 pg. 1-sec. B, pg. B12.

Rolfsen, Bruce. "Ready or Not, Noble Eagle missions are taxing F-16 Pilots so much that 1 in 4 of them may not meet combat qualifications-and they're not alone," *Air Force Times*, 4 March 2002, p.14-18.

Ricks, Thomas E. "Military Overhaul Considered, Rumsfeld Eyes Global Command for Terrorism Fight," *Washington Post*, 11 October 2001, pg 1-3. Internet. Available from: http:// ebird.dtic.mil/Oct2001/e20011011military.htm accessed 19 October 2001

"Debate Swells Over Sending Unarmed Troops to Guard U.S. Borders" *Inside the Pentagon*. March 7 2002. Internet. Available from: //ebird.dtic.mil/Mar2002/e20020307debate. Accessed 10 March 2002.

"Military Resists Domestic Role" *Government Executive*, Vol 33 Issue 14 (Nov 2001) : 28.

"Rumsfeld Envisions New Command Responsible For Homeland Security," Inside The Pentagon, 17 January 2002. Internet. Available from: http:// ebird.dtic.mil/Jan2002/e20020117envisions.htm. Accessed 17 January 2002.

U.S Government Reports

Bush, George H. W. *Public Report of the Vice President's Task Force on Combatting Terrorism*, Washington D.C.,: U.S. Government Printing Office, 1986.

Department of Defense, *Quadrennial Defense Review Report*, 30 September 2001. Washington D.C.: DTIC, U.S. Government Printing Office, 2001

FEMA, United States Government Interagency Domestic Terrorism Concept of Operations Plan. Internet. Available from http://www fema.gov/r-n-r/conplan.pdf; Accessed 26 January 2002.

_____. in Coordination with the Catastrophic Disaster Response Group "An Assessment of Federal Consequence Management Capabilities For Response to Nuclear, Biological, or Chemical (NBC) Terrorism, A Report to the President" (February 1997)

_____. The Federal Response Plan (FRP) April 1999. Internet. Available from: http:// www. fema.gov/r-n-r/frp/. Accessed 15 November 2001.

General Accounting Office, Report to Congressional Requesters. *Combating Terrorism, Federal Agencies Efforts to Implement National Policy and Strategy (GAO/NSIAD-97-254)* Washington D.C.,: U.S. Government Printing Office, 1997.

_____. *Opportunities to Improve Domestic Preparedness Program Focus and Efficiency (GAO/NSIAD-99-3)* Washington D.C.,: U.S. Government Printing Office, 1998.

_____. *Combating Terrorism, Threat and Risk Assessment Can Help Prioritize Target Program Investments (GAO/NSIAD-98-74)* Washington D.C.,: U.S. Government Printing Office, 1998.

_____. *Combating Terrorism How Five Countries Are Organized to Combat Terrorism (GAO/NSIAD-00-85)* Washington D.C.,: U.S. Government Printing Office, 2000.

_____. *Combating Terrorism, Issues to be Resolved to Improve Counterterrorism Operations (GAO/NSIAD-99-135)* Washington D.C.,: U.S. Government Printing Office, 1999.

_____. *Homeland Security challenges and Strategies in Addressing Short-and Long –Term National Needs (GAO/T--02-160T)* Washington D.C.,: U.S. Government Printing Office, 2002.

_____. *Combating Terrorism, Need to Eliminate Duplicate Federal Weapons of Mass Destruction Training (GAO/NSIAD-00-64)* Washington D.C.,: U.S. Government Printing Office, 1998.

_____. *Combating Terrorism, Need to Eliminate Duplicate Federal Weapons of Mass Destruction Training (GAO/NSIAD-00-64)* Washington D.C.,: U.S. Government Printing Office, 1998.

The United States Commission on National Security/21ˢᵗ Century (Hart Gary and Rudman, Warren [co-chairmen]) The United States Commission on National Security/21ˢᵗCentury "Road Map for National Security: Imperative for Change*" The Phase III Report of the U.S. Commission on National Security/21ˢᵗ Century*, Washington D.C.: Government Printing Office 15 February 2001.

Executive/legislative/DOD Actions, Orders and Directives

Department of Defense Directive. "Military Assistance for Civil Disturbances (MACDIS)" *DoD Directive no. 3025.12,* 4 February, 1994. Internet. Available form: http:// www. dtic.mil/whs/directives/corres/html/302512.htm. Accessed 10 February 2002.

_____. "Military Support to Civil Authorities (MSCA)" *DoD Directive no. 3025.1,* 15 January, 1993 Internet. Available form: http:// www. dtic.mil/whs/directives/corres/html/30251.htm. Accessed 10 February 2002.

_____. "DoD Cooperation with Law Enforcement Officials" *DoD Directive no. 5525.5,* 15 January, 1986. Internet. Available form: http:// www. dtic.mil/whs/directives/corres/ html/55255.htm. Accessed 10 February 2002.

_____. "Military Assistance to Civil Authorities (MACA)" *DoD Directive no. 3025.15,* 4 February, 1994. Internet. Available form: http:// www. dtic.mil/ whs/directives /corres/html/ 302515.htm. Accessed 10 February 2002.

U.S. Congress. *The Robert T. Stafford Disaster Assistance and Emergency Relief Act*, P.L. 93-288, as amended, P.L. 100-707, as amended, 42 USC 5121, et seq. Internet. Available from: www disastercenter.com/Stafford. Accessed 1 April 2002.

U. S. President. Presidential Decision Directive. " PDD 39 U.S. Policy on Counterrorism" 21 June 1995. Internet. Available form: http:// www.fas.org/irp/offdocs/pdd39.htm Accessed 15 December 2001.

U. S. President. Presidential Decision Directive. " PDD 62 Combating Terrorism" 22 May 1998. Internet. Available form: http:// www.fas.org/irp/offdocs/pdd-62.htm Accessed 15 December 2001.

U. S. President. Presidential Decision Directive. " PDD 63 Critical Infrastructure Protection" 21 June 1995. Internet. Available form: http:// www.fas.org/irp/offdocs/pdd/pdd-63.htm Accessed 15 December 2001.

U. S. President. Presidential Decision Directive. " PDD 63 Critical Infrastructure Protection" 21 June 1995. Internet. Available form: http:// www.fas.org/irp/offdocs/pdd/pdd-63.htm Accessed 15 December 2001.

U. S. President. Homeland Security Presidential Directives-1-3, *Organization and Operation of the Homeland Security Council, Combat Terrorism Through Immigration Policies,* and *The Homeland Security Advisory System.* Internet Available from:http://www.fas.org /irp/ offdocs /nspd /hspd-1.htm. [hspd-2, hspd-3] Accessed 20 March 2002

U.S. President. *Executive Order Establishing Office of Homeland Security.* (EO 13228) 8 October 2001. Internet. Available from: http:// www. whitehouse.gov/news/ releases/ 2001/10 /print / 20011008-2html Accessed 25 October 2001.

U. S. President. Homeland Security Presidential Directive-2, *Organization and Operation of the Homeland Security Council.* Pg 1. Internet Available from:http://www.fas.org /irp/ offdocs /nspd /hspd-1.htm. Accessed 20 March 2002

U.S. Senate. Permanent Sub Committee on Investigations of the Committee of Government Affairs *Global Proliferation of Weapons of Mass Destruction, Hearings* , Part III, March 27, 1996, Sentencing Statement of Judge John Duffy.

Manuals/Doctrine

U.S. Department of Defense, Office of the Chairman, Joint Chiefs of Staff. *Joint Electronic Library* [CD ROM], February 2000.

_____. Joint Publication 0-2. *Unified Action Armed Forces*, Washington D.C.: Government Printing Office, 24 February 1995.

_____. Joint Publication 1-02. *Department of Defense Dictionary of Military and Associated Terms*, Washington D.C.: Government Printing Office 12 April 2001.

_____. Joint Publication 3-0 *Doctrine for Joint Operations*, Washington D.C.: Government Printing Office, 10 September 2001.

_____. Joint Publication 3-01.1 *Aerospace Defense of North America* Washington D.C.: Government Printing Office, 4 November 1996.

_____. Joint Publication 3-07 *Joint Doctrine for Military Operations Other Than War (MOOTW)*, Washington D.C.: Government Printing Office, 16 June 1995.

_____. Joint Publication 3-08 *Interagency Coordination During Joint Operations Volume I*, Washington D.C.: Government Printing Office, 9 October 1996.

_____. Joint Publication 3-08 *Interagency Coordination During Joint Operations Volume II*, Washington D.C.: Government Printing Office, 9 October 1996.

_____. Joint Publication 3-57 *Joint Doctrine for Civil Military Operations* Washington D.C.: Government Printing Office, 8 February 2001.

Department of the Army, Headquarters. Field Manual 100-1. *The Army*. Washington D.C.: Government Printing Office, June 1994.

_____. Field Manual 3-0. *Operations*. Washington D.C.: Government Printing Office, June 2001.

_____. Field Manual 3-07 (DRAG). *Stability and Support Operations*. February 2002. Internet. Available from: http:// www. cgsc.army.mil/cdd/FM307/fm307.HTM. Accessed 26 February 2002

_____. Field Manual 100-19. *Domestic Support Operations*. Washington D.C.: Government Printing Office, July 1993.

Speeches/Interviews

Richard Cheney, "Vice President Cheney Delivers remarks at the 56th Annual Alfred E. Smith Memorial Foundation Dinner" (speech given at the Waldorf-Astoria Hotel, N.Y.C.18 October 2001) Internet. Available from: ww.whitehouse.gov/vicepresident/.com Accessed 5 January 2002.

Donald Rumsfeld, interviewed by Sam Donaldson, "ABC News This Week" 16 September 2001.transcript Available form Federal News Service Inc.

Roten, Colonel (USMC) Deputy Commander JTF-CS , Telephone Interview conducted by Tim McAteer 12 March 2002. Fort Leavenworth, Kansas.